Becoming A Counselor:

The Light, the Bright, and the Serious
2nd Edition

Samuel T. Gladding

Becoming a Counselor:
The Light, the Bright, and the Serious, Second Edition

10 9 8 7 6 5 4 3 2

American Counseling Association Foundation
5999 Stevenson Avenue
Alexandria, VA 22304

Cover and Text Design
Martha Woolsey

Library of Congress Cataloging-in-Publication Data

Gladding, Samuel T.
Becoming a counselor : the light, the bright, and the serious /
    by Samuel T. Gladding.
    p. cm.
    Includes bibliographical references.
    ISBN 978-1-55620-281-0 (alk. paper)
    1. Counseling.   2. Counselors.   I. Title.

BF637.C6G525 2008
158'.3—dc22   2007044481

DEDICATION

To Thomas J. Sweeney

*An active and strong voice for counseling as a profession,
the founder of Chi Sigma Iota (counseling academic
and professional honor society international),
a friend and mentor*

TABLE OF CONTENTS

Preface xi
About the Author xiii

Section | One
BEFORE COUNSELING: PERSONAL GROWTH   1
1.   Choices: Holding On or Letting Go 3
2.   Milledgeville 5
3.   The Rock Beneath the Ivy 7
4.   Just as I Am 9
5.   Cool Breeze: A Lesson in the Tragedy of Racism 13
6.   I Married the Football Team 15
7.   Judge Hardy 17
8.   A June Night in December 19
9.   How the Past Came Into the Present 21
     Points to Ponder 22

Section | Two
INITIATION INTO THE PROFESSION   23
10. The Calling 25
11. Encountering the Unexpected: Bandits 27
12. "Uh-Huh" Is Never Enough 29
13. The Locked Ward 31
14. From the Inside Out 33
     Points to Ponder 35

Section | Three
FINDING WHAT WORKS   37
15. Talk Is Cheap 39
16. Tex Ritter Smith 41
17. Playing Hunches 43
18. Consultant or Catalyst 45
19. Sometimes It Is How You Ask the Question 47
20. Three Acres of Garlic 49
21. The Music of Life 51

Table of Contents

22. Knowledge Is Power Up to a Point 53
     Points to Ponder 55

Section | Four
LEARNING FROM FAILURE   57
23. Sleepy Time Client 59
24. Bo: A Disaster in Assessment 61
25. Rabbits 63
26. Testing a Theory: The Sound of Silence 65
27. Chipmunk Cheeks...67
28. The Right to Struggle.......................................71
29. Be Modest 73
30. A Door, a Phone, a Window.............................75
31. The Price of Being Ill Prepared 77
32. The Wrong Side of Presentations 79
33. Learning the Lingo 81
34. The Wake-Up Dream 83
35. Love on an Academic Level............................85
36. The Spanish Inquisition or How Not to
     Write a Resume..87
     Points to Ponder 89

Section | Five
SKILLS AND PROCESSES   91
37. The Basics 93
38. The Difficulty of Change 95
39. The Pace of Change...97
40. Boundaries: An Awakening.............................99
41. Modeling: A Case of Starlings 101
42. Mr. TBA: The Importance of Knowing Others 103
43. Empathy 105
44. Afraid of Blood 107
45. Omelets...109
46. The Concrete Counselor 111
     Points to Ponder 113

Section | Six
CREATIVITY IN COUNSELING   115
47. Socks 117
48. The Foxhole...119
49. Pantomime Can Be Powerful 121
50. The Phony Prisoner...123

51. The Words Are There/I Don't Know Where..................125
52. Nothing Could be Finer ... Almost! 127
    Points to Ponder 130

Section | Seven
MULTICULTURAL AND SPIRITUAL CONSIDERATIONS   131
53. An Encounter With the Klan 133
54. Shirley...135
55. WASPs 137
56. The Argentine..139
57. Spirits, Spirituality, and Counseling....................141
58. Becoming a Student of Culture............................143
59. Putting on the Gloves With Mother Teresa 145
60. Getting There 147
61. Ten Pesos for the Gringo 149
62. Geography and Identity...................................151
63. Women Are People!..153
    Points to Ponder 155

Section | Eight
THE INFLUENCES OF COLLEAGUES, FRIENDS, AND FAMILY   157
64. The Office...159
65. Happenstance: Note Whom You Quote 161
66. Sources Within 163
67. Cool Under Fire 165
68. Scars...167
69. Courtland, the Turkeys, and Me in Knoxville,
    Tennessee 169
70. Parenthood...171
    Points to Ponder 173

Section | Nine
WORKING WITH GROUPS AND FAMILIES   175
71. The Other Side of Labels 177
72. The Power of Nancy Drew..................................179
73. Airtime..181
74. Three's a Crowd But Four's a Family
    Counseling Session.......................................183
75. Sex Therapy: The Challenge...............................185
76. Drama Break..187
77. An Unexpected Reconciliation: Laura Ashley...............189
78. Humor 191

Table of Contents

79. Research and a Reframe Within the Family 193
80. Words Alone 195
    Points to Ponder 196

Section | Ten

PROFESSIONAL DEVELOPMENT   197

81. Supervision 199
82. Court: The Rules of the Game 201
83. Research and Theory: A Reminder From Carl Rogers 203
84. My Pal Sal 205
85. Adjectives and Adverbs 207
86. A Quiet Riot: Life as an Oxymoron.............................209
87. Thunder, Turmoil, and Thoughts.................................211
88. Who Wants to Work? 215
89. Not by Work Alone 217
90. Rejection..219
91. Counselors Anonymous 221
    Points to Ponder 222

Section | Eleven

DEVELOPMENTAL CONSIDERATIONS   223

92. Aging But Not Developing 225
93. Tree With Lights..227
94. The Unforgettable New York Adventure 229
95. Don't Take It Literally..233
96. Erotic or Erratic: What a Difference a Word Makes 235
97. Attitudes 237
98. The Wearing of Black and Development 239
99. Lost 241
100. Just Because You're the One and Only Doesn't Mean
     You Won't Be Left Cold and Lonely.............................243
101. Resiliency and Unpredictability 245
102. Finding a Vision That Works...247
     Points to Ponder 249

Section | Twelve

LEADERSHIP   251

103. The Human Side of Leadership: Being President
     of the American Counseling Association..........................253
104. Dealing With the Press Can Be a Mess—
     But You Should Do It..259
105. The Leader as a Catalyst and Servant..............................263
106. Leadership in Counseling After a Crisis.........................267

107. Smoke and Mirrors 273
     Points to Ponder 274

Section I Thirteen
ISSUES IN COUNSELING   275
108. Counseling as a Quiet Revolution...............................277
109. Counseling in an Age of Chaos: Learning From a
     Historical Perspective 279
110. Counseling in Context: Keeping a Balance 283
111. Diagnosis, Labels, and Dialogue..................................285
112. Forgiveness Is Transformational....................................289
113. The "isms" in Counseling 291
114. Territory Folks Should Stick Together 295
115. Counseling or Counselling: Internationally Speaking 299
116. Why Counseling?...301
     Points to Ponder 304

Section I Fourteen
TERMINATION   305
117. The Quilt 307
118. Hair..309
119. Avoiding Permanent Termination: Self-Care and SIFLs....311
120. On Grief and Gratitude 313
121. Always Becoming 315
     Points to Ponder 316

Epilogue 317
Notes 319
References 321

PREFACE

Some events change your life. Most are not so powerful. Critical occurrences that have an impact are landmark experiences such as leaving home, the death of a parent, the achievement of a goal, failure, an accident, a chance encounter, or a natural disaster. Other transitional times may be less notable but still influential, such as moments of insight, prejudice, or simple acts of kindness. Outside of these memorable incidents, the rest of our existence is rather mundane and routine. Thus, we may be at a loss to recall what we ate or to whom we talked two days ago because neither was significant in life-changing or life-giving ways.

In counseling we see people at crisis points. They are usually ready or willing to make necessary changes, some of which are dramatic. However, as clinicians we seldom remember most of the people we encounter because the helping process is more routine than avant-garde. My experiences reflect that pattern. I can recall only a few of the hundreds of individuals I have assisted. Yet, some events in my personal and professional life have been turning points that have influenced my growth and development in a manner similar to those situations that have most affected my clients. You have had (or most likely will have) some similar experiences. These times are filled with a plethora of emotions and thoughts as well as new behaviors.

The vignettes in this text are representative of many universal dimensions involved in becoming a counselor and helping professional. In these stories, you will find examples of

- the light, that is, the humorous aspects of life and counseling;
- the bright, that is, the insightful nature of life and counseling; and
- the serious, that is, the deeper and more sobering parts of life and counseling.

Sometimes these three dimensions occur simultaneously and are obvious. Sometimes they are sequential and subtle. Regardless, they are a part of the experience of both novice and veteran counselors.

Although the incidents in these stories are unique, they are also broad based. You may find yourself identifying with them and their applicability to you. The "Points to Ponder" section at the conclusion of each section is an especially good place for such reflections. In any case, it is my hope that this book will assist you in living a richer, fuller, deeper, and more meaningful life through gaining insight into yourself and the processes involved in the bittersweet process of choice and change.

In reading this text, remember that some incidents represented here, mainly those that occurred in my own life, are true. However, most of the stories in this book are based on facts that have been altered or embellished a bit. Thus, in all circumstances, characters who are a part of these episodes (unless specifically identified) have been disguised through multiple means such as being combined with similar people in a composite, having their names changed, having their genders switched, or having their presenting problem modified.

There are a number of people who have been pivotal in the publication of this book. Clients, colleagues, and situations are the key sources for what appears on these pages. However, the one who has done the most to transpose my reflections into readable prose is Anita Hughes, my former assistant at Wake Forest University, who initially helped organize and edit much of this material. I could not have completed the task without her. My colleagues in the Department of Counseling at Wake Forest University, especially Donna Henderson, Debbie Newsome, Laura Veach, Tom Elmore, Pamela Karr, and John Anderson, have also been most supportive. Erin Binkley and Elizabeth Cox, my graduate assistants in 2006–2007 and 2007–2008 respectively, offered invaluable insights as well. I am likewise grateful for the positive input into my life by Thomas J. Sweeney, to whom this book is dedicated, and the encouragement and constructive comments of Carolyn Baker, Director of Publications at the American Counseling Association (ACA). My gratitude is also extended to Rich Yep, Executive Director of ACA, and to the publication committee members of ACA who reviewed and favorably recommended this work. Finally, I am indebted to my wife, Claire, and our children, Ben, Nate, and Tim, for the rich memories they have provided me in regard to counseling and life. Becoming a counselor is a continuous and challenging process.

—*Samuel T. Gladding*

ABOUT THE AUTHOR

Samuel T. Gladding is a professor and chair of the Department of Counseling at Wake Forest University in Winston-Salem, North Carolina. He has been a practicing counselor in both public and private agencies since 1971. His leadership in the field of counseling includes service as

- president of the American Counseling Association,
- president of the Association for Counselor Education and Supervision (ACES),
- president of the Association for Specialists in Group Work (ASGW),
- president of Chi Sigma Iota (counseling academic and professional honor society international), and
- vice president of the Counseling Association for Humanistic Education and Development (C-AHEAD).

Gladding is the former editor of the *Journal for Specialists in Group Work* and the ASGW newsletter. He is also the author of more than 100 professional publications. In 1999, he was cited as being in the top 1% of contributors to the flagship journal of the American Counseling Association, the *Journal of Counseling & Development,* for the 15-year period from 1978 to 1993. Some of Gladding's most recent books are *The Counseling Dictionary* (2nd ed.; 2006), *Counseling: A Comprehensive Profession* (6th ed.; 2009), *Group Work: A Counseling Specialty* (5th ed.; 2008), *Counseling as an Art: The Creative Arts in Counseling* (3rd ed.; 2005), and *Family Therapy: History, Theory and Process* (4th ed.; 2007).

Gladding's previous academic appointments have been at the University of Alabama at Birmingham, Fairfield University (Connecticut), and Rockingham Community College (Wentworth, North Carolina). He was also Director of Children's Services at the Rockingham County (North Carolina) Mental Health Center. Gladding received his degrees from Wake Forest University (B.A., M.A.Ed.), Yale University (M.A.R.), and the University of North Carolina at Greensboro (Ph.D.). He is a National Certified Counselor, a Certified Clinical Mental Health Counselor, and a Licensed Professional Counselor (North Carolina). He is a member of the North Carolina Board of Examiners in Counseling.

Gladding is a Fellow of the American Counseling Association and the recipient of other numerous honors, including

- the American Counseling Association's Gilbert and Kathleen Wrenn Caring and Humanitarian Person Award,
- the American Counseling Association Foundation's Bridge Builder Award,
- the Association for Creativity in Counseling Lifetime Achievement Award,
- the Association for Spirituality, Ethics, and Religious Issues in Counseling Humanitarian Award,
- the Chi Sigma Iota Thomas J. Sweeney Professional Leadership Award,
- the C-AHEAD Joseph W. and Lucille U. Hollis Outstanding Publication Award,
- the ACES Professional Leadership Award,
- the ASGW Eminent Career Award, and
- the North Carolina Counseling Association's (NCCA) Ella Stephen Barrett Award for leadership and service to the counseling profession.

Dr. Gladding is married to Claire Tillson Gladding and is the father of three children: Ben, Nate, and Tim. Outside of counseling, he enjoys tennis, swimming, music, and humor.

BEFORE COUNSELING: PERSONAL GROWTH

Templeman/Gladding travels in me
a restless presence, a history
of time and people who walked the world
long before my birth.
Attuned to the sound of their stories
I wince at their failures
and bask in their glories.
Knowing I journey on my own
I am aware that I am never alone
for they are a part of my life.

No one begins life as a counselor. We develop into professionals over time. With or against the currents of our environment we steer, drift, or proceed toward becoming counselors instead of economists, historians, or English scholars. Part of the reason has to do with our early personal history and with circumstances in life.

I am no less a product of the time, environment, and interpersonal interactions than anyone else. I was born two months after World War II, the third and youngest child of Russell and Gertrude Gladding, who were Virginians in heritage but Georgians geographically. My childhood was spent on Church Street in the Atlanta suburb of Decatur. Besides my parents, my older sister, Peggy, and brother, Russell, and my maternal grandmother, Pal, lived in our three-bedroom, one-bath house.

As an infant, I had dislocated hips that required a body cast and several operations to correct. In addition, I came into the world with a dislocated left elbow, a couple of missing bones in my hands and feet, and shortness of stature. It was discovered a little later that I had a central auditory processing disorder that manifested itself in not being able to accurately distinguish the sounds in words. That made spelling, writing, and learning a foreign language a nightmare. I also had cavity-prone teeth. So life as a child and adolescent was challenging and often discouraging.

My family was religious, and having a consistent and personal relationship with God became a strong thread in the fabric of my existence. I grew up thinking I wanted to be a minister like my maternal grandfather for whom I was named.

The nine stories that follow will give you a glimpse into my childhood, but they are meant not to focus so much on me as to open your mind to thoughts of your early experiences. Some of the stories are funny, while a few are tragic. They all deal with human nature and personal interactions. In each of the vignettes there is knowledge that you may have learned in a different way than I did. Ask yourself as you read: What forces in your developing years influenced you to be who you are now?

chapter 1

Choices: Holding On or Letting Go

Whenever someone asks me if I have a good illustration of a situation involving choices, I smile and quickly respond. I'm not sure why I smile (it probably has to do with reflexes). I do know why I respond. I have a rather graphic illustration.

It happened during the exploratory preschool time of my life. My older brother, Russell, and his friends were climbing up to the rafters of a neighbor's garage. I wanted to be with them but I could not climb the ladder on the inside of the structure.

Seeing my plight, my brother and his merry band of playmates tried to be helpful. They threw down a rope from above and told me to tie it around me. I did so awkwardly but enthusiastically and with great anticipation. Then the group in the rafters started pulling in order to lift me up. All went well for about 10 to 15 feet whereupon the rope slipped. Such slippage would have been fine in most cases, but the place where the rope slipped with considerable force was around my neck. Unbeknownst to my brother and his friends, they were hanging me.

The good news is that within a few seconds my brother looked down (in horror, no less) and saw the noose and my beet-red face. He had to make a split-second decision as to what to do as he realized what was happening. With my head almost to the top of the platform where it and my body would have found a solid surface, he made a fateful decision. "Let him go," he yelled, "or we will kill him."

Being about 20 feet off the ground by then I wanted to reply: "But if you choose to drop me, you may also end my life." Unfortunately because my windpipe had been closed off, I could not say anything. Windless and limp, I followed the force of gravity to the ground, which was actually a concrete driveway. The trip down was quick (although it seemed like an eternity and could have made that word a part of my history). Before anyone could say "Farewell," I made the sound of a thud, like a sack of potatoes being dropped from a roof, and the back of my head hit the cement!

At that point my brother hurried down the ladder, looked me over, unloosened the noose, and quickly ran home swearing to my mother that he had nothing to do with what she was about to behold. My head was like a coconut cracked open with a stone. The only difference was that blood began pouring out rather than coconut juice and while coconuts are silent, I burst forth with a scream. Neighbors came running, dogs began barking, babies stopped crying, and my grandmother, from four houses away, made the innocent and objective remark to my mother, that it sounded like someone was dying (which was more true than she knew). A neighbor carried me home to my visibly shaken mother, who got another neighbor to drive her to the doctor with me in her lap, my head wrapped in towels, thus looking like a Middle East sheik. Two hours later I returned home with a dozen stitches, a pound of gauze, a headache, and a much calmer maternal unit. All ended well. I even acquired a souvenir where the hair never grew back—a bald spot!

Therefore, when someone asks about situations involving choices, especially those that are avoidance–avoidance, I do not think about the devil and the deep blue sea. Instead, I think about hanging around or falling down. Neither is a course I wish to take again. Ironically, what ended up in a mess started out with the best of intentions. Clients we see in counseling who appear to be just marking time may not be too far away from trying to avoid choices, especially hard ones, like my brother and his friends faced. They may think that they will be on solid ground if they do nothing or suspend their decision making. As counselors we need to be ever mindful of the dynamics involved in making choices. If we do, we will not just be more knowledgeable, we will be wiser and more empathetic. We will also be better able to help our clients struggle through the decision-making process so that the crucial decisions they make will not fall flat.

chapter 2

Milledgeville

"Behave or they'll send you to Milledgeville!"

My friends and siblings would often say that when I was growing up and acting what they termed "a little bit crazy."

The reason the name of a former capital of Georgia came up in conversations was that it was the site of the Georgia Insane Asylum. No longer was Milledgeville a place where you went for politics. It was now a place you were sent because you were a "lunatic."

I never went there, but I am aware that during the time of my childhood, the institution was overcrowded. Five thousand patients were confined in a space constructed for half that many. I have since learned that the book and movie *The Three Faces of Eve* (about multiple personalities) was based on a person who spent part of her life at the asylum.

In some ways I wish I had been sent to Milledgeville because it seemed so mysterious. However, I am more grateful that I did not take that ride south. I would probably have been traumatized.

I do not know of any sentence I have heard since my preteen years that has made me act more properly than the one that began this piece. Behavior has consequences whether it sends you somewhere or not.

chapter 3

The Rock Beneath the Ivy

I knew better. And I knew that I knew better. And my friends knew that I knew better. But there I was on top of the horse stables—30 feet up above the ivy down below with my friend Carl Jones saying, "If you want in the club, jump."

Being 11 at the time, I wanted in the club (whose name I have now forgotten). And so, looking straight ahead, I sprang from the roof like I was diving from a platform and flew through the air gracefully for a millisecond. Then I landed with a thud and with considerable pain. Most of my body was fine. However, below my right elbow was a rock that simply obeyed the laws of physics and homeostasis. In other words, it did not move, and when my elbow came crashing down upon it, the hypothesis that bones are not as hard as granite was proven once again. My elbow, though pointed, did not break through the rock. Instead, it was shattered and so was my hope of landing on my feet metaphorically or literally.

At first the grown-ups thought I had a sprain or a bruise, even though Carl's dad was a doctor (an allergy specialist, I later found out). The long and short of the story is that the elbow was never set properly, and I lost full rotation in it. After the accident, I found it difficult to eat with my right hand. Therefore, I switched and became more ambidextrous by using my left hand to hold my fork or spoon. I already was a lefty when batting in baseball.

Thus, the mobility I lost on one hand gave me new agility on the other. I wish I had not had the accident and did not still carry some physical pain in my right elbow.

Sometimes the breaks we get in life are not what we want. Yet they can lead us to become more flexible and remind us never to foolishly leap or seek after the superficial.

chapter 4

Just as I Am

rowing up Baptist was mentally and theologically challenging for me—at least in my childhood church where the emphasis was on record keeping, recitation, and evangelism. Every Sunday morning, each child present (and the adults, too) had to fill out a record form checking such categories as "on time," "read lesson," and "brought Bible." There was a chance to have perfect attendance and to score 100% as well! In addition to the records, there was a focus on memorizing scripture, most of which was from the New Testament, Psalms, and Proverbs. As far as I know, I was never asked to recite anything from the Song of Solomon.

I did fine in the first two categories of being a 1950s Baptist—keeping a record of my attendance and memorizing scripture. However, the third emphasis, evangelism, seemed a bit irrelevant to me until one summer day when the weather and our minister both got hot. I was 12 years old and seated with my family in the 11 a.m. worship service in the fifth row on the left hand side of the sanctuary. It was a place that our family claimed for years. On that summer Sunday when the sermon ended, the minister gave the traditional invitation for anyone who wished to come forward and join the church as the congregation sang "Just as I Am."

Several verses were sung and no one came. Therefore, the minister asked everyone to bow their heads and close their eyes while the choir sang the hymn slowly and with feeling. He said he was sure the Lord was calling someone that day but he was not sure exactly what they were being called for. I was pretty sure the Lord did not have my number so I relaxed a little bit. However, after the choir had sung and no one had responded, the minister asked the congregation to sing some more. Two, then three, verses were sung. Still there was no one in the front of the church except the preacher. Maybe the Lord had dialed over to the First Presbyterian Church that morning. At least that thought entered my mind.

Appearing to me to be somewhat frustrated, out minister asked for the head-bowing, eye-closing response again while the choir sang softly in the background. When his expectations were not met, he said to the congregation's surprise,

"I want everyone who has volunteered to be a missionary to the Congo to come to the front."

"Sam," he said, "that's you and Sandra," pointing to one of my friends who was the same age as me.

I was stunned but began to make my way to the aisle past my parents and siblings who seemed a bit shocked that I was being called to Africa. Coming down the aisle towards the front, I saw my friend, Sandra, who was a pretty girl with long blond hair, blue eyes, and a smile that could melt the heart of almost any 12-year-old boy. But this morning, she was not radiant. She was not smiling. She looked as if she was upset, and to make matters worse, she was crying. The tears ran down her face in small streams, eroding her makeup significantly and causing her mascara to run down her cheeks. When I asked why she was so distressed, she sobbed out with significant feeling, "I don't want to go to the Congo as a missionary!"

"I'm not too wild about the idea myself," I replied in one of the great understatements of my life.

Nevertheless, we made our way to the front where the pastor had us stand in line and be greeted by anyone who so chose to come by after the service.

Well, because of the time that had been taken up with the invitation, most people chose to hurry home to what in the South was a traditional large Sunday noonday meal. Only a handful of the faithful came to shake our hands and wish us well as we stood there in disbelief. Unfortunately, one of the most ardent of the faithful was at the front of the line. It was "Miss Thelma," an elderly woman who was in church every time the doors opened. She was a great supporter of foreign missions and shook our hands so vigorously that I found my whole body vibrating and shaking.

"God bless you children," I remember her saying while thinking "God is probably the only one who can bless us and I really wish the Almighty would make us invisible right now."

Had the story ended there, I would have been humiliated and humbled but happy. However, the rest of my teenage years and into college was influenced by this bizarre Sunday event. For as old as I thought Miss Thelma was, she was not old enough to stop coming to church and asking me how my preparation to serve in the Congo was coming along. Every Sunday during the school year, I would see her and she would ask me Africa questions, such as what was the capital of Liberia, where was the Horn of Africa, and was the Ivory Coast a place where there were a lot of elephants. Over time I became pretty good on African geography and history. Also, over time I developed to the point where I was able to go off to college and I did—300 miles away!

At that juncture in my life, Miss Thelma had truly grown old and a bit senile. Nevertheless, she kept coming up in my life and would inevitably find me whenever I was home for breaks. She assumed by the time I was 18 that I was in Africa and only home on furloughs (which seemed too frequent and regular in her mind). She asked me how my missionary work was going and since I was a Georgian at a North Carolina school, I interpreted her question broadly, telling her that I was doing my best to minister to the heathen who surrounded me daily. I assured her the uneducated were being taken care of. She would smile and then walk away.

As the years went by, Miss Thelma became frail and weak. Sandra got married and moved away. I eventually changed denominations and became a United Methodist. Although my awareness of myself and others increased a lot from being called forward to the front of my church that fateful Sunday, most of what I learned came later. It specifically manifested itself in the form of being able to think quickly on my feet and to memorize a lot of facts about a distant continent. I finally went to South Africa in 2006, but as far as I know Sandra never went any further geographically than Savannah. I doubt either of us will ever be missionaries at this juncture in our lives, but I am sure the memory of that Sunday morning will dwell in our minds forever.

The Lord certainly works in mysterious ways and understanding what happens, when, and for what reason is not necessarily something that we ever are privileged to know. I doubt I will ever solve the mystery of that moment so many years ago. It does seem to me, though, that when people are allowed to make their own decisions, they enjoy life better and are potentially more spiritual. Not everyone needs to be volunteered for service in the Congo, and there are a lot of Miss Thelmas in the world!

chapter 5

Cool Breeze: A Lesson in the Tragedy of Racism

*I*n high school I was a football manager. That basically meant taking care of the team's equipment, taping ankles before games, and cleaning up after the players went home. On Saturday mornings during the season, it meant straightening up the locker room as well as doing some of the team laundry. While we waited for the dryers to finish, my fellow managers and I would play games of touch football out on the field that had been the center of attention the night before. Sometimes we played among ourselves, all White boys from the Atlanta suburb of Decatur. At other times, African American kids would join us and prior to the integration of our high school, we would have a spirited interracial game.

My favorite player on either side of the ball was a 15-year-old African American kid about my age known as "Cool Breeze." He earned the name because of his speed. He was faster than anyone else. Whether going up the middle or around the end, we seldom were able to catch him, let alone stop him. Instead, he would dart pass and afterward we would feel the "cool breeze" of the air he had stirred up. In a word, he was "awesome!"

As great as Cool Breeze was on the field, his life and success were later not as great. The reason is he did not have choices educationally, socially, and vocationally. He was relegated to a lifestyle that restricted his movement and ambition because of segregation. What could have been, never was. The mindset of the day kept people "down" and prevented possibilities. Whenever I think of the time, it makes me sad and mad. Life is too valuable to waste and individuals are too important to treat like chattel. If there is one thing counseling can do and one reason I am a counselor, it is to open up possibilities for those who, because of background or circumstances, have not had opportunities. While opportunity does not guarantee success, without options people almost always fail.

chapter 6

I Married the Football Team

I was never picked on in high school. Maybe one reason is that I took precautions. I married the football team (and later one of their players in what was described as a "womanless wedding"). Yes, as mentioned in Chapter 5, I became a football manager from my sophomore year on. For a guy who was 5 foot 3 and 115 pounds, the move was sheer finesse. After all, in the 1960s, football was popular in Georgia. To be their best, football players relied on managers for everything from getting good equipment to getting a proper pre-game ankle taping. Therefore, managers were treated favorably. Instead of depending on a guardian angel to protect me from those who might have thought of picking on me, I relied on about 50 guys who were considered the biggest, strongest, and toughest in the school environment.

The arrangement worked well. I went out of my way to supply members of the team with whatever they needed. Many of them, in turn, hung out with me before, during, and after school. As an extra insurance policy, although I did not need it, I became the athletic editor of the yearbook my senior year. Did I have friends? Well, at least I did not have any overt enemies. Plus, I had a lot of fun both on and off the field, whether it was packing and carrying equipment or picking and placing photographs with just the right captions for the annual.

I look back on those years and activities with pleasure and intrigue. No one told me or even encouraged me to get close to the biggest and strongest guys in the high school. It was just something I did because I knew on an instinctive level that it would offer me safety. Vicariously, it gave me a chance to participate in a dramatic game that I would never play except virtually and on an informal basis.

Over the years I have watched other people do similar things in regard to their environments. It is as if most of us have a feel for what will work in our lives. The difference between those who succeed and those who do not, I think, is a willingness to trust themselves and take a risk that they might be right. When that does not happen, individuals often become alienated from themselves and from others.

Judge Hardy

$\mathcal{A}$lthough I never felt particularly small growing up, I realized pretty early in my life that I was vertically challenged when compared with other boys. I did not measure up to them in height. However, even in childhood I competed, which is the game that boys play regardless of age. I had some success in adolescence as an athlete, mainly in tennis, and I made above-average grades at school. I dated and I was generally popular with my classmates because of my sense of humor. At the same time, I looked for heroes because I realized most of the people who were seen as leaders in the late 1950s and 1960s did not look like me. They were primarily tall, rugged, and handsome. Think John Wayne on one end of the spectrum and John F. Kennedy on the other.

Whether it was luck or just plain serendipity, I found my hero one Sunday afternoon as I watched a 1930s Judge Hardy movie with my family. The two prominent actors in the film were Mickey Rooney and Judy Garland. I knew nothing about them as people. What I did notice is that they were attractive young people and that Mickey Rooney did some pretty cool things in the movie, as the son of Judge Hardy, a wise, older man. In addition, Judy Garland seemed to really like him. She was pretty, perky, and his girlfriend. So how could I lose if I acted like Mickey Rooney? My father was not a white-haired judge so I could only pretend he was. Likewise, my family was not as cool as what I saw on the screen before me, but I could imagine. Thus, much of what I did in high school and even early in college was based on the model of a fictitious family and environment.

Years later I read about the tumultuous and tragic lives of Mickey Rooney and Judy Garland and wondered to myself how I could have formulated part of my identity based partially on who they portrayed. At the same time I realized that it was the character roles in the Judge Hardy movies to which I was aspiring. I identified with a short-statured adolescent, Andy, who was played by Mickey Rooney. Likewise in youth, I looked at Judy Garland as Polly and saw the positives she personified. I was fortunate not to have too much information too soon. Otherwise, I might have become cynical, morose, and lost.

It is the same with our clients. They need to develop at their own pace, not ours. They need role models and may find them serendipitously and in places where we might never have imagined. Not knowing may keep them going and on track to discovering aspects of themselves they would otherwise miss.

chapter 8

A June Night in December

When I was 17 (going on 18), as is true with many male adolescents, I was infatuated with a young woman and yet scared to death to ask her for a date. Her name was June and she was 16 (going on 17). I found her warm name and personality inviting. Best of all, she lived just a couple of blocks from my parents' house. So one December day, I mustered up all my boyhood courage, walked over to her at school, and asked her to "The Snow Ball," a wonderfully exciting dance in December that was completely misnamed since we lived in Georgia. To my delight, she accepted.

On the night of the grand occasion, I picked June up at her house and after chatting with her folks for a few minutes, we made our way to the car. I could tell that romance, rather than any frozen precipitation, was in the air. Her eyes were as dilated as mine must have been and that is probably the reason for what happened next.

I opened the car door for June and after she slipped in gracefully, I closed the door behind her with a flare and quickly, yet lightly, walked around to my side of the car (knowing I was on the street where she lived). After getting in, I looked over at her, expecting romantic glances and maybe even a kiss, but to my astonishment she was crying.

"Oh no," I thought. Like any 17-year-old boy I did not know what to do when a girl cried. I had been assured by Frankie Valli and the Four Seasons on the radio that "Big Girls Don't Cry" and I thought June was a big girl. However, I had sense enough to ask what was wrong since her tears had sobered me up enough to realize that this "enchanted evening" just might be different from what I had planned.

"Why are you crying?" I asked. "Are you filled with emotion and riveted with thoughts of you and me?"

"No," she sobbed.

"Did you just think of something unpleasant?" I queried.

"No," she insisted.

"What is it then?" I finally said in an open and inquiring manner.

"You just slammed the car door on my hand!" she blurted out.

And sure enough to my dismay as I looked up I realized that not only had I slammed her hand in the car door but it was still caught there. Therefore, like an Olympic sprinter, I was out of my seat, on my feet, and around to try to relieve the pressure faster than you could say "Emergency Room" which is where we ended up that night.

As embarrassing as this time was, it was not the end of my relationship with June. When she got the bandages off, I visited and wrote her sappy poetry. She liked the attention and her hand finally healed. I still come in contact with her, but she still keeps her distance, as if I might handle the occasion in the wrong way again. Now, however, we can laugh at the folly and faux pas of that night.

In reflection, I look back occasionally at that time—a hard night that still gives me chills. In it is a memory of teenage awkwardness and growth. June is a reminder that the way to a young woman's heart is not through her hand! However, events that go wrong can turn out better in the long run than they appear at first. That goes for mistakes we make in counseling as well as blunders we make in life. Time and attention to aspects of our life that are hurt or shattered can do much to make them better.

chapter 9

How the Past Came Into the Present

I was named for my maternal grandfather, Samuel Huntington Templeman, who was among other things a prominent Baptist minister in Winston-Salem, North Carolina, in the 1930s. I grew up thinking I wanted to be a minister like him. He was apparently a very good man. Once when he was pastor of a church in South Carolina, he prevented the lynching of an African American man.

My maternal grandfather, who was born 20 years after the end of the Civil War, was a Virginian. He graduated from the University of Richmond, but instead of staying in the South where he would have been safe and welcomed, he finished his theological education at Colgate-Rochester Divinity School and Columbia University. Going North was a bold move because feelings between the North and South were still tense when he went. However, he thought he would be a better person and a more effective minister if he left his region for awhile and got to understand other people and ways of life.

After I graduated from Wake Forest University, I too went North and attended Yale Divinity School. I felt that if my grandfather could do it in a time of tension, I could do it in a time of relative calm. I did not end up being a minister or saving anyone's life in a dramatic way. However, I think getting outside of my region of the South helped me to become a more understanding person and relate to other people better. I owe a debt to my grandfather for giving me the courage to go beyond the safety of the world in which I grew up and get beyond my zones of comfort.

Points to Ponder

1. When have you ever faced a dilemma of holding onto a situation or letting it go? What did you do? What were the results? How do you think your experience then influences your counseling and personal decisions now?

2. Who did you most identify with growing up? What did you learn from that person? How is that person you admired still manifested in your life?

3. How has your family's history made an impact on you for better or worse? How does your family's history still have an impact on you today?

INITIATION INTO THE PROFESSION

In a world full of dreams
you must listen to the beat
of the durm
that is your heart

—Gladding, © 1993[1]

We all begin our journey to be counselors as people who are seeking a purpose greater than ourselves and for the benefit of others. In the process, we often find a new awareness of who we are and what we can and should do. Our progress of becoming is a paradox at times. The more we let go of the roles that have confined us, the greater freedom we have. Our flexibility also increases. Yet, in this awareness, we realize that much of whom we are developing into is linked to what we have inherited in both our personal and our professional histories. We are different from our professional ancestors, but their legacies assist us in learning the art of helping others and ourselves.

In the five vignettes in this section, I have highlighted some learning that took place early in my career. On a personal level, the stories are about discovery of both self and methods of assisting others. On a professional level, these brief snapshots are about growth and insight that not only are unique in these particular situations but also have universal qualities.

chapter 10

The Calling

*T*he sun was low in the sky as I hit the Washington, DC, beltway. I was driving from New Haven, Connecticut, to Atlanta, Georgia, in a 1968 Mustang and was fighting fatigue and the glare off the windshield. Other cars were passing me by, and I wondered if life might not be doing the same unless I made an adjustment and shifted gears. I was a second-year student at Yale Divinity School, and through a self-assessment of my thoughts and feelings over the past few months, I had realized I was not going to be divine, let alone a minister. Although that revelation may seem minor now, it was a major epiphany for me in the spring of 1970. I had had a plan for 21 years to follow in my maternal grandfather's footsteps. I had been named for him, grown up on Church Street, and been a member of a very religious family. The agenda was loaded. I always thought I would spend my Sunday mornings behind a pulpit (most likely standing on a Coca-Cola crate) but definitely not sitting in a pew, sleeping late, or going to the lake. Now, reality had set in, and I was headed south both literally and figuratively.

Yet, as fate would have it that day, I did not make it all the way to my parents' home in Atlanta. Instead, I wound up spending the night in Winston-Salem, North Carolina, the city that was the home to my undergraduate alma mater, Wake Forest University. So the next morning, before completing my journey, I decided to visit the campus and the former Dean of Students, Dr. Tom Elmore, an administrator I had known and trusted for a number of years. Tom had recently resigned the Dean of Students position to start a counselor education program. After exchanging pleasantries, I told him of my struggles, and with his best attending skills, he listened. Then he said five words that changed my life: "Why don't you try counseling?"

Not realizing that he meant that maybe I should seek personal or career counseling, I thought he was implying that I should enroll in a counseling program. The next fall, having finished Yale, I matriculated into the counseling program at Wake Forest. It was a move filled with the instant recognition that the profession would be my psychological home for life . . . and it has been.

chapter 11

Encountering the Unexpected: Bandits

*I*t was a hot summer afternoon in North Carolina. I was driving down rural roads to my first job in a mental health center following the morning of my graduation. With a Master's of Counseling degree in hand, I was sure that little stood between me and success other than the 50 miles from the city of Winston-Salem to the little town of Wentworth. On that June day I took in the scenery and daydreamed. However, my euphoria was disrupted by an unexpected event along the way. There before me, in hand-painted letters, were these words on a signpost: "Bandits—Straight Ahead."

"Holy Lone Ranger!" I said to myself. "Where am I going, and will I get there in one piece?" (My new employer had failed to tell me that I might encounter some mid-route turbulence on the way to work.)

Nevertheless, out of curiosity and in trepidation, I continued. As I drove I saw other equally crude but well-constructed signs informing me of the presence of bandits—15 miles, 10 miles, 5 miles, 1 mile, and finally "just around the corner." In a gallows humor I muttered anxiously to myself, "If it pays to advertise, these guys are going to make a killing." Thus, as I drove the last few hundred yards, I did so knowing I had been forewarned.

To my relief, however, what I encountered around that last bend in the road was not dangerous. Rather, it was a dilapidated wooden building, badly in need of repair, with a bundle of items piled out in front and a banner over the door that read, "Cheap! Cheap! Cheap! My brother steals and I sell it. Welcome to Bandits!"

While I passed up the opportunity to go view what was hot (and what was not), the memory of that day has stayed with me over the years. The reason, I think, is the impact and message of the road signs that I read. What they conveyed outwardly and what was displayed ultimately was a dichotomy. Similarly, when we meet with clients, we may receive initial signs that do not reveal the reality of their lives. On such occasions, the experiences we have turn out differently than anything we would ever have imagined on our way to work.

chapter 12

"Uh-Huh" Is Never Enough

*M*y initial education and credential as a counselor was a master's degree. I did my practicum/internship in the campus counseling center in a Rogerian, person-centered fashion. I said "uh-huh" long before the late Ray Charles and Pepsico ever thought it was the right thing to do in their commercials of the late 1990s. Amazingly, my clients got better, and when I left the center I carried Rogerian techniques and great optimism with me to the rural mental health facility where I was initially employed. I was the "uh-huh counselor," and I was ready to heal the world. My expectations of becoming another Carl Rogers quickly and dramatically faded, however, the first week of my employment when I realized that "uh-huh" is never enough.

The case that awakened me came on the Friday of the first week of work. All during the week preceding that event, my main job had been to learn how to play cards with clients who were severely disturbed. Growing up in a strict Baptist home with a mother who was a PK (preacher's kid), I had never been allowed to possess playing cards, let alone play card games. I am sure the director of the mental health center thought that learning such games would be good for me and the clients who came to the center to play on a regular basis. At first it was fun, but I grew restless as the week wore on.

I was tired of dealing (and losing) and anxious to see real neurotic people who I thought needed my services. Sure enough, at 4:59 p.m. on the first Friday of my career, a call came to the center from a social service agency that was requesting help in an emergency. I was standing by the secretary when the call came in, awkwardly shuffling cards in my hands out of a sense of boredom while simultaneously shuffling my feet slowly in anticipation of an opportunity. As the conversation dragged on, I shuffled my feet faster as the secretary introduced my availability to deliver services to the people at the agency in a way I will never forget.

"All our good people are seeing clients right now," she stated. "However, we do have a new person we just hired. He's kind of green and I don't know much about him except he's not very good at playing cards. However, if you are really desperate we will send him over. Are you really desperate, ma'am?" The reply was affirmative, and before the secretary and the person she was speaking to could say "Jokers are wild," I was off to the agency about five miles away.

When I arrived I was courteously and skeptically greeted and told that the person I was going to see was literally banging his head into the wall in a room at the end of a hallway. I was offered the opportunity to have someone from the agency go into the room with me if I requested. But I assured everyone that this case was fairly routine in mental health circles (after my introduction by the secretary, I was afraid to admit I hadn't a clue as to what to do). So I entered the room feeling a great kinship for Daniel in the lion's den and yet realizing faith, in this case, would probably not pull me from the jaws of my inadequacies or deliver me from my pride.

To make a long story short, what I found in the room was a middle-aged man with long shaggy hair and faded blue overalls knocking his head quite hard against a cinderblock wall. My previous training would have told me to be empathetic and probe by saying something like "How does that make you feel?" or to reflect and say something like "I hear your head going thud, thud, thud against that wall pretty regularly. Tell me about that."

However, I was more direct and behavioral and stated "I'm from the mental health center. If you really want help, stop doing that."

He looked at me in a sheepish, stunned manner (as if to say, "Why didn't somebody say that about 20 minutes ago?"), and amazingly enough, he quit.

Sometimes being direct and specific can help you and your clients be realistic and get better. The theory I entered that situation with was alright but my client was all wrong for it. The next semester I enrolled in my first behavioral counseling course. I also listened to my clients even more closely after that, especially their nonverbal language.

chapter 13

The Locked Ward

Having worked for a mental health center for a few months, I was informed that I and "Nurse Nancy" would regularly start visiting clients from the county who were at the regional mental hospital. The idea was to help them begin to make a transition back to our community. It seemed interesting, and I noticed with amusement that the coffee they served at the hospital was poured into Mellaril cups.

"Nothing to fear," everyone assured me. "Just look straight ahead, trust the experience of the personnel on the locked wards, and stick with more seasoned professional colleagues" (such as, in this case, the nurses). So I entered my first locked ward, close to the side of Nurse Nancy, looking stern like an Army commando and quietly saying repetitively under my breath the 23rd Psalm and the Boy Scout motto.

All went well for about 10 feet. Then a wild-haired woman from the back of the ward spotted us and with loud shouts and angry motions started coming toward us. I looked to Nurse Nancy for reassurance, but I quickly noticed her eyes were glazed over like a Krispy Kreme donut, and she had what is known in the clinical literature as "tonic immobility." (I could have probably used a gin and tonic myself then, but there was no time.) With the woman closing in and no help in sight, I decided to survive by grabbing the keys from my colleague and escaping. There was just one problem. Nurse Nancy was as rigid as a two by four, and being frozen in fright, she was not about to release the keys that would have given me freedom.

Thus, I did the most prudent thing I knew—I ran. I was faster than the woman (thank goodness), and there were strategically located support beams on the ward that I could use to run around and wear her out. Finally orderlies arrived (I now know why they call them orderlies) and peace was restored. Nurse Nancy, still clutching the keys, and I then departed unceremoniously. I was wiser and a bit more frazzled and fatigued than when we arrived. But I also realized the absurdity of what had just happened.

From that experience I learned to stay flexible in counseling and never passively depend on a co-counselor to make the situation better. I also came to realize that sometimes your best asset in counseling may not be your words but your actions, in this case behavior involving my feet. Finally, I learned anew how close the comic and the tragic are to each other. I could have been hurt if I had remained immobile. Instead, by keeping my head and using my legs, I was able to put distance between the woman and me and ultimately to place the incident in perspective.

chapter 14

From the Inside Out

W hen we emphasize growth we are often enlightened and gain unexpected insight. That fact came home to me one day when I lived in Connecticut. At the time, I had a professional friendship with an older man by the name of Art Lerner. He lived in California and had double Ph.D.s in literature and psychology. Art had taken me on as a "project" after I had made a professional presentation at a convention in which I had mentioned his name and one of his books. He wanted to teach me everything he knew and I was anxious to grow. He would sometimes call and talk to me about everything from probability to the use of theory in counseling. Subtly, he was teaching me about human nature. Then one day he called and asked, "Could you meet me in the city? I'm coming to New York to see my agent."

Well, before you could say "I want to be a part of it," I said "yes" and on the appointed day of his arrival I took the train into the city and met him at Grand Central Station. I did not have an agenda but he did. He had made luncheon reservations at the United Nations for us where we saw both interesting people and had a delightful and inexpensive meal. Then it was on through the subway to his agent's apartment, where I met an elderly, bent-over woman with blue hair and a cane whose living quarters were chock full of books and filled with the aroma of freshly brewed coffee and chocolate chip cookies. Amid the clutter and smell, much discussion occurred between Art and his agent, whom I shall call "Agnes." Since I was not involved directly in their conversation, I nibbled on cookie crumbs, drank coffee, and caught a glimpse of how the high-powered world of New York publications really worked. I was both impressed and intimidated.

As we were about to depart, however, Agnes looked at me for what I thought was really the first time and asked pointedly, "So are you going to write, too?"

I was surprised by her query. I reflected momentarily and then hesitantly replied that I did not think I had lived long enough to have any experiences that were worth sharing with others.

"Then you must think again," my hostess countered. "You must be a person who knows the depth of his soul and the width of the world. You need to go inside as you go outside. Then you may realize who you are and you may write."

Her words caught me off guard. I had no reply. Rather, I walked with my friend back to the train station while catching glimpses of my breath in the cold, darkening air. There I boarded the train towards New Haven and looked out the window at the frosted countryside. Silently, I pondered my interaction with Agnes during the long ride home.

Since that day, I have wondered if the words conveyed during my brief conversation with a woman I hardly knew might have some universal dimension to them of what it is "to become"—to grow. I am still caught up in her words that "you must go inside as you go outside to realize who you are." I doubt I will ever be free from that sentence.

Points to Ponder

1. What is the story of your becoming a counselor? Was it a planned and systematic process or a result of happenstance?

2. What theory do you ascribe to most closely? Can you imagine a situation in which it was inadequate or not appropriate? What then would you do?

3. When have you ever been surprised by the unfolding of events? What did you learn in that situation?

FINDING WHAT WORKS

He changed,
giving her small compliments at breakfast, such as
"I like the way your hair looks" or
"Nice dress."
She wondered,
"What's he doing?"
but she also knew she liked his words.
So as the days continued
she responded to his acts of kindness
with new behaviors of her own.
He changed;
She changed;
They changed.
And it was for the better!

—Gladding, © 1996[2]

When I began my work as a counselor, I was somewhat sure I knew what worked. I had taken a course under Rollo May and attended lectures by Carl Rogers, Albert Ellis, Virginia Satir, and other notable therapists. Therefore, I was surprised when I struggled sometimes with certain clients whose problems these masters had made look somewhat easy to resolve.

- Was it me?
- Was it the theory I was using?
- Was it the client?

- Was it all of the aforementioned factors combining in a dynamic way that my texts, counseling films, and teachers had not explained?

I was not sure.

However, I began to realize in time that I could not really emulate any one of the greats I admired. My clients were different from theirs. I was a person whose history and knowledge also differed. So, from insight came a struggle to take calculated risks and interact with clients in ways that were uniquely my own. In the process, I found interventions that worked and gained confidence and competence. It is in finding what works that we sometimes find our identity and humanity.

chapter 15

Talk Is Cheap

From the adamant behaviorist on my doctoral committee at the University of North Carolina at Greensboro (as well as from my clients), I have learned that sometimes an altered action is worth a thousand words. The most blatant example of the power of new behavior occurred in my professional life with a woman who was literally doing nothing in counseling. I would meet with her, and she would ramble. I would confront her rambling, and she would be evasive, explaining to me that she needed to give me details so I could truly understand her. I would then listen again, and she would repeatedly stray. Our sessions seemed to go on forever, and at the end of each, there was nothing to show for the time invested.

Finally, one day in trying to understand the dynamics that were occurring in our sessions, I told her that I thought she was not making progress and that I was concerned. She replied flippantly that she thought counseling was fairly worthless and ended by saying, "And besides, talk is cheap."

I looked at her, somewhat amazed, dazed, and befuddled. I was not particularly offended by the fact that she did not seem to highly value counseling. However, her last statement made me think that I needed to make an intervention so that her perception would have an opportunity to be modified. Thus, I decided to take a risk and an action that I normally would never have considered.

"I'm doubling your fee," I told her.

Well, if you live near Cape Canaveral you know about the noise and fire associated with the launching of rockets. And if you had been in my office that afternoon you would have thought several missiles had taken off from a non-Florida site. The volume and flow of words in our session increased dramatically, and my client came close to blasting off with anger. However, along with a pick up in the sound and heat came a focus in her sentences. She now knew that time was costly, that life does not continue on one course forever, and that language and thoughts can be powerful if directed toward a goal. From that point on, she took off in a direction that had purpose and resulted in her defining and reaching a destination that allowed her to live a more fruitful, exciting, and inviting existence.

Had I taken no action, I can only surmise that she would have stayed stuck, gotten sick, or continued off course in her life. Change came in the form of doing something differently.

chapter 16

Tex Ritter Smith

One of the lightest and yet most anxious moments in my counseling career came about the time Debby Boone was singing "You Light Up My Life." You may remember that song, but chances are if you do that you are now trying to forget it. But at the time of the song's initial popularity, I was a counselor in a county mental health center that was housed in a pre-Civil War building that Sherman forgot to burn.

One day at the center, a rather large mountain of a man named Tex came in for his first appointment. What made him a bit unusual was the fact that he had a gun in a holster strapped to his side. I was upstairs in my office, but my faithful secretary, Sa-rah (she actually pronounced her name "Say-Rah," not Sarah), quickly let me know that Tex and his six shooter had arrived. She was disturbed, and I must admit I had concern, too.

Nevertheless, I came downstairs to find Tex in the waiting room. I introduced myself, shook his hand, and then said to him as he stood up,

"You know, Tex, we don't allow firearms in our counseling sessions. They have a way of frightening the counselors. However, we can arrange to take care of your gun while you and I talk. Come with me."

I then took him over to Sa-rah's desk, gave her one of those knowing winks that means "play along with me here," and said to Tex, "Sa-rah, our receptionist, used to be a cowgirl. She's from the West you know. Sa-rah, tell Tex where you are from."

Without blinking an eye or seeming to understand anything that was going on, Sa-rah said in a rather monotone voice, "I'm from Mayodan, North Carolina."

Trying to put a good spin on her answer, I replied: "Yes, Mayodan, North Carolina, where the Mayo and Dan Rivers converge, where the deer and the porcupine play, where seldom is heard a discouraging word or any sounds other than wild animal noises. You know, Tex, some people say that Mayodan is where the West really begins. There are no buffalo there, but they do have an ostrich farm. Tex, have you ever tangled with an ostrich?"

Unimpressed, Tex just grunted.

"There's no rapport being built here," I thought, but I continued the conversation, giving Sa-rah a double wink (like help me out a little here will you, Sa-rah, or we both may die). Then I told Tex that Sa-rah would give him a receipt for his gun.

"She does it for people who have poodles, opossums, or other possessions that we think would be better left out of sessions," I said.

Well, as Tex reached for his gun, Sa-rah just stared into space, so I gave her hand motions to start writing something. Finally, she reached for a pink telephone message pad, and as Tex laid down his gun, Sa-rah handed him a pink slip of paper with these words on it:

"While you are away, this is where your gun will stay."

Tex seemed okay with the note, and as luck would have it, we actually had a good session. He never showed up with his firearm again.

From my experience with Sa-rah and Tex that day, I learned that sometimes if you stay fluid and keep the conversation light until it needs to be heavy, you can set up the right conditions in counseling so that your encounters can be productive. Being flexible as a counselor in the midst of potential danger and difficulties means "keeping a grip" on yourself and others and not "shooting from the hip." It involves timing, patience, and a sensitivity to know that most solutions in life come from interactions that are mindful but ones you would probably never have predicted.

chapter 17

Playing Hunches

I wish counseling were purely scientific. If it were more like physics or chemistry, I would be sure of what to do and when to do it. I could use a formula. But because of the gap in research and practice, we, as counselors, must sometimes use our intuition as much as our cognitive knowledge.

That realization occurred to me one day when I was visiting a hospitalized client who was going to have a major operation the next morning. We talked for some time at his bedside about what he had been through therapeutically and what his expectations of the future were. It seemed to me that he had a solid knowledge of reality.

As I was leaving, he said, "I'm not at all worried about tomorrow."

His words made perfect sense. Yet, I was uncomfortable with them. I did not know the reason behind the discomfort, but it was there. Then it dawned on me. It was not what was said but how it was said. My client's words had come out in a bravado manner that made me suspect that he was not as sure of himself as he had conveyed.

Therefore, I made a 180-degree turn in the doorway and reentered the room. "Tom," I said, "while I do not doubt your sincerity, I do have a hunch that what you just said doesn't ring true in your mind."

He laughed for a minute and dismissed my observation with a glib remark or two, but then reaching out for my hand, he confessed, "You're right."

In the next half hour, my client's thoughts and emotions came together. When I left I knew he was not just pretending to be brave when he said he hoped to see me the next day. Yogi Berra, the legendary New York Yankees catcher and coach, once purportedly made the statement that "you can see a lot through observing." He could have also said, had he been a counselor instead of a catcher and coach, that "you can hear a lot just by listening," especially if you listen for feelings.

chapter 18

Consultant or Catalyst

A consultant is sometimes referred to as someone who blows in, blows off, and blows out. Occasionally, that is true. However, good consultation happens when a counselor is not self-centered but instead works with someone else for the benefit of a third party, for example, a client or an organization.

When I worked in a mental health agency I was frequently asked to consult at one of the four local school systems. The asking became so burdensome that I realized I needed to do something to maximize time and effort spent in working with school personnel. Therefore, I invited each of the school systems to send their counselors to the mental health center for a meeting once a month. My thought was that the counselors as a group could help each other and I could orchestrate that process as well as add to it by being a consultant. The plan worked initially. Then some of the more anxious and overwhelmed counselors began to dominate the meetings by asking questions concerning some severe situations.

In order to remedy the situation, I asked our in-house psychiatrist to join the group. At first I thought the group might try to use him like a local advice giver, but instead of seeing him in such a narrow way, they opened up and queried him about a wide range of disorders and dysfunctions. Everyone was fascinated and pleased with the interactive nature of the discussions, and soon there was a request that our monthly meetings become biweekly. They did, and as they expanded so did the topics covered.

What I noticed out of all of this effort was that I was no longer receiving as many telephone calls or requests to come out to the schools. I also noted counselors gaining greater diagnostic skills and assessment abilities. Furthermore, the counselors in the group became better at working with each other and at formulating plans for the children and parents who populated their offices. They frequently consulted with each other.

I became a catalyst in the process of being a consultant. The psychiatrist and the counselors had been brought together. Their interactions were dynamic and far-reaching. They became greater than the sum of their parts. They grew in knowledge and ability. Everyone won.

chapter 19

Sometimes It Is How You Ask the Question

One of those aspects of counseling that I have become attuned to over the years is the importance of how a question is worded and to whom. Open-ended questions are usually best in eliciting thoughts and feelings, whereas closed-ended questions are most appropriate for obtaining specific information. Likewise, children and those who may be a bit mentally challenged do better with simpler inquiries. However, there is no specific formula for what question is asked and how it is worded. I have found out this fact on numerous occasions, but I will illustrate it with two stories.

My initial experience in realizing the importance of how you ask questions came with a late-adolescent girl who was brought into counseling by her mother. The mother was concerned that the girl was being promiscuous and was going to get into serious trouble. I could see why the mother would get such an idea because of the way her daughter was dressed. A low neckline and a high hemline were invitations for trouble at her age, especially given the fact that she was flirtatious. However, I did not want to appear to side with the mother immediately and thought I needed to say something to the girl in order to establish rapport. Trying to begin on a positive note, I asked, "Jenny, what do other people say is your most outstanding quality?" Without blinking, she replied, "I'm 115 pounds of romping, stomping sex."

Her response was accurate but not what I was looking for so I countered, "Besides sex, Jenny, what is your best quality?"

That question resulted in an answer that was more productive, but by then both she and I were in the doghouse with her mother and my face was scarlet.

Another time, I also made a probe that could have been better phrased. I was getting ready to lead a group, and I thought I would ask my wife, Claire, a question I was going to use in the group to see how it would work.

"Honey," I said, "what group in your life gave you hope?"

"The Eagles," she replied in a straightforward manner.

Before I could explain to her that I was not talking about rock-and-roll groups (which I frequently did around the house), she said, "Yeah. It was their song 'Desperado' that really spoke to me. Those lyrics that 'you better let somebody love you before it's too late' made me wake up more to my life and my relationships. Aren't you glad?!"

Well, I was glad because the song had entered her life before I did and probably had a positive impact on the development of our relationship. Yet, it was not quite what I was looking for when I asked the question. So, the next day as I began the group I made a clarifying statement as such: "Besides a singing group, what group in your life gave you hope?"

The responses were much more of what I had in mind, and the outcome of the group was good because the question had been refined and tailored.

chapter 20

Three Acres of Garlic

I normally greet clients by introducing myself, shaking their hands (if appropriate), and asking them to tell me something about themselves. All usually goes smoothly. However, once after the introduction and handshake, my client, a rather burly man, said, "I just want you to know that I'm as strong as three acres of garlic."

I thanked him for the information and sank back in my green-cushioned chair wondering where to begin. So I said,

"Mr. Garlic, what brings you here?"

He was not humored and replied, "I hate my wife. She's been having an affair. I caught her, and I've now thrown her out of the house. I'm thinking about what to do next. I want revenge."

To put it mildly, I'm convinced that revenge is every bit as strong as love. I am also aware that trying to dissuade someone from seeking revenge directly is often not profitable (even though it is a legally prudent action). So in this case, I asked my client to explain the details around his thoughts and tried to stay cognitive and factual with him. He was unclear about what he was going to do, which was a good sign. Nevertheless, I also had him promise not to do anything violent until he saw me the following day. Then I asked him to do some homework for the next day.

"Find someone else who has been hurt in a love relationship," I said, "and tell me what the person did that helped."

The assignment was a gamble because there are many negative models, especially in movies, who resort to less than productive behaviors when they get hurt. I was equally afraid that he might pick up on some less than positive country music and decide to never get over his pain. The next day, however, when my client arrived he had a CD in his hand.

"Here," he said, "play this song."

To my surprise, the CD was by Don Henley, and the song he asked me to play was "Heart of the Matter." As the song progressed, the emotions in my client increased. They finally broke in a cascade of tears when Henley sang, "But I think it's about forgiveness, forgiveness, forgiveness, even though you don't love me anymore."

The words spoke to my client's pain and simultaneously gave him an option for acting that he would not have readily accepted from me. My client followed his heart in listening to his feelings, but he took his lead for constructive action from a singer who verbalized emotions and talked about a way out of despair—"forgiveness."

Just as the literature in counseling reminds us, sometimes the best we can do is to be aware of what we cannot do. Such a realization may help in assisting our clients find alternative resources for themselves by looking into books, movies, and music that promote positive interactions and solutions.

chapter 21

The Music of Life

I once worked with a young man who played the guitar for a hobby. I asked him in our intake if there was anything he wanted to say with the guitar because his speech was limited. He said he would think about it, and in the next session, he came in with the guitar and simply said, "Listen."

Then he played some of the most dramatic music I have heard from a guitar. It started off quietly but reached a crescendo that was loud, off-key, and unsettling.

"That's my life," he said after the piece was concluded.

Seizing the moment, I replied, "On which note would you like to begin?"

He picked a section most on his mind at the time and we were off. He would play and then talk. We would look at variations on themes, tunes that sounded similar, and the rhythmic or arrhythmic quality of his selection. He would try some new chords on occasion and vary the beat of a piece. For weeks he brought in his guitar, and we worked through his life as depicted in music. Interestingly enough, not only did the music become mellower in our sessions, but he came to be in greater harmony with his surroundings—and himself—as well.

In the celebration that ended our final session, he again said, "Listen." As I did I could not help but smile as he gleefully played and sang with great feeling the song Frank Sinatra made famous, "My Way."

chapter | 22

Knowledge Is Power Up to a Point

nce in my career, I taught psychology in a small college in what can only be described as a rural and somewhat remote part of the state in which I was living. One of those courses in which I gave instruction was abnormal psychology—a class always filled to the brim with fascinating material and curious students, some of whom too often displayed the traits on which I was lecturing. One young man, whom I shall call "Anonymous," particularly stands out in my memory of those times because of his language patterns, his rather well-intentioned but bizarre actions, and what he taught me about change.

To give you a brief glimpse of the young man in question, I will simply say that he tried to talk as if he were hip and often used the word *man* as a preface to opening his remarks. He almost seemed a throwback to the 1960s, but I taught him much later. Regardless, after a particularly intense class on mental disorders and families, he approached me with an excited and seemingly enlightened facial expression. I thought maybe he would comment on the intricate nature of some of the research we had covered, but alas, my initial hopes were dashed.

"Man," he said, "I learned a lot today."

I smiled confidently (silently giving myself a compliment and a pat on the back) as I stood before him, hands across my chest, trying to look wise.

"I don't know if you know it," he said, "but you described my family today."

I winced a bit in my mind, shuffled my feet back and forth, and assured him I did not know any of his relatives.

"No problem, man," he said, "I now am aware that I live in an abnormal household with really messed up parents and a sister who is just bizarre. I am going home tonight to tell my family what is wrong with them."

Before I could get a word in edgewise, like "don't," he wheeled around and with the speed of a sprinter, he had gone down the hall, through the doors, and into what I felt like was certain trouble.

The next day, my worst fears for the young man seemed to have materialized. I saw him in the halls looking bedraggled, dazed, and downcast. His backpack seemed full, and his face was flushed. Trying to find out what had happened and to simultaneously establish rapport, I approached him slowly and said,

"Man, how'd it go with you and your family yesterday?"

He looked up at me and with a slight smile that reminded me of colleagues of mine in the Army who had been in the heat of combat. He then replied, "Fine, fine, fine—at first."

"Yeah, man," he continued, "I went in there and told my father he was paranoid, schizoid, and had a character that was disordered. Then I confronted my mother with the fact that she was histrionic, inadequate, and in the words of Linda Ronstadt, I yelled 'you're no good, you're no good, you're no good, mother, you're no good.' Finally, I went in my sister's room and told her she was mentally challenged, unstable, and a disgrace to the human race. Yeah, man, I really let them have it."

Then he paused and looked down.

"So, man," I said, "what happened next?"

Sheepishly he said, "Well, man, I'd really prefer not to tell you, but man, do you know anyplace where I can live? They kicked me out of the house."

Knowledge is power, but in the young man's case he became confused about what to do with the limited power he possessed. Knowledge is best when it is used to help people become aware of and sensitive to who they are in regard to others as well as who others are in reference to them . . . and what reality is.

Points to Ponder

1. When have you found it better to listen than to talk? Be specific in fleshing out an example.

2. Write down several open-ended questions and the answers you would expect to receive. Ask the questions of a few friends and observe whether any of the questions need to be refined.

3. When have you found comfort or support in listening to music or reading a book? How did you use what you learned?

LEARNING FROM FAILURE

She went about kissing frogs
for in her once-upon-a-time mind
that's what she had learned to do.
With each kiss came expectations
of slimy green changing to well-bleached white.
With each day came realizations
that fly-eating, quick-tongued, croaking creatures
don't magically turn to instant princes
from the aftereffects of a fast-smooching,
smooth-talking, helping beauty.
So with regret she came back from a lively lily pond
to the sobering stacks of the village library
to page through the well-worn stories again
and find in print what she knew in fact
that even loved frogs sometimes stay frogs
no matter how pretty the damsel or how high the hope.

—Gladding, 1976[3]

No one likes to fail or taste the bitterness of defeat. Yet, in losing sometimes we gain. I have found that true in a number of arenas in life, including counseling. On the one hand, it is humbling not to live up to the standards that you have set for yourself as a professional. On the other hand, it is human. At such moments, there is an opportunity not so much to criticize oneself but to constructively learn.

Learning From Failure

The stories in this section are all about learning. The experiences were hard lessons but ones that have stayed with me and stood the test of time. They may be similar to events you have had or will have, but hopefully you can "go to school" through reading this material and not repeat the mistakes I made. Part of being an effective counselor is preparation, but even the most prepared counselor encounters the unexpected. Ask yourself as you read these vignettes how, if you had been the counselor, you could have avoided making the missteps I did. Also query yourself as to ways you could ethically interact with the situations presented in these snapshots of sessions and slices of life.

chapter 23

Sleepy Time Client

I once worked with an accountant as a client who was incredibly dull. He would come and talk about his relationships in such detail that I found my mind drifting. Therefore, I used to take two cups of strong coffee into our sessions. One was for me. The other was for him in case he began boring himself. As fate would have it, one day the appointment was on, but the coffee pot was off. I had cups but no java. There we were, my client and I, face to face, with no stimulants to help us.

I tried. I really made an effort to stay awake and to be active. I moved around initially and used every technique I knew. But finally his monotone, flat-affect voice, and his propensity for using 10 words when one would do, wore me down. Before you could say "deep sleep," I had sunk into the comfort of my chair only to be awakened by my own snoring.

As I woke up in a startle, I could see he was not pleased. I was, to say the least, extremely embarrassed. I thought of saying, "My kids kept me up late last night and I am tired," or trying to appease him by saying, "I'm sorry and you don't have to pay for today's session."

However, believing that honest self-disclosure can be powerful and productive, I made a confession.

"Ralph," I said, "I regret having gone to sleep during our session. I have never gone to sleep during a counseling session before. This is truly a first. But, Ralph, if I did this while trying to listen, I wonder what might be happening in your other relationships where people are not necessarily attempting to be so close."

He looked at me, and to my surprise, he quietly said, "I really don't have any other relationships. That's why I'm here. When I tell you I have friends, they are mostly mental. I am lonely. I am unloved. And I want to stop fooling myself and you."

From then on, the details stopped and the feelings started. I did not have to depend on the coffee pot, and Ralph did not have to depend on me to be his friend. The sleep of embarrassment woke up both of us to new possibilities, thanks to honest and appropriate self-disclosure.

chapter | 24

Bo: A Disaster in Assessment

art of my life as a counselor has been spent doing assessments. Some of these assessments have been completed in the offices in which I worked, whereas others have occurred in a school environment. I must confess to liking my office better than school environments because I have found there is no standard place to test in some schools. I have also realized over the years that rapport and relationships (not to mention scores) are sometimes negatively affected when I am on the road.

The most sobering experience I had in this regard was with a first grader whom I shall call "Bo." He was a light-skinned African American child with a wiry build. The principal brought him to me and said he wanted Bo assessed because Bo did not seem able to settle down like the rest of the children and do his lessons. I had my standardized testing instruments with me, but I did not have a place to test. Therefore, I asked in the presence of Bo (because he was already there) where we were to conduct the assessment. The principal had not really thought ahead. However, he led us to the nurse's office, which was a glassed-in area that had the nurse's name on the outside of the door and was furnished with a bed, a desk, and two chairs. It would have to do. With that he left.

I immediately recognized the difficulty of the environment and the fact that Bo did not know me. Therefore, I thought I would try to establish rapport and create a positive atmosphere before I did anything else. I told Bo who I was and what we would be doing. I also asked him to tell me about himself (but at age six he had nothing to say).

Realizing the nonverbal nature of young children, I said, "Bo, I have a puppet here in my materials I want to show you." Then I reached down and behind me to retrieve the sock puppet I had brought for such occasions.

The next thing I heard was the sound of a slamming door. Bo had bolted and was literally running down the hallway bouncing off the walls in a zigzag fashion like a ball in a pinball machine. I was shocked but instantly on my feet. I quickly opened the door and tore down the halls running after Bo. He was easy to follow because of the sounds he was making and the course he was taking, but he was fast and the chase seemed to go on forever. I finally caught Bo in front of the principal's office where the principal was standing, watching these actions unfold. He was not pleased nor were the teachers who came into the halls to see what had happened after hearing Bo blow quickly past their classrooms in a disruptive manner. I was exhausted and I knew Bo was, too, so we ended our session that day. Fatigue had taken its toll.

Driving back to the office with the memories of the time, I thought that before I entered a school again for an evaluation I would call first to make sure they had a place for me to set up. I also knew that in advance of seeing a child (or an adult for that matter) for an assessment, I would be sure I had sufficient background information and would not depend on disinterested personnel to find a place for me to work. I realized that materials used in an evaluation from sock puppets to scoring sheets should always be as close as possible and preferably out in front or to the side of you. Bo taught me many lessons!

chapter 25

Rabbits

I had completed intake information on a man and asked him what he would like to work on in the session. He looked at me a bit negatively and simply stated, "I am not talking until you get rid of the rabbits in this room."

We were in a rural area so I surveyed our surroundings. Not seeing any rabbits, I asked where they were. He pointed to an imaginary hare (that I assumed was wild), and I went over, grabbed it by its invisible ears, then opened the door, and threw it outside. As I went to sit down he pointed to a second nonvisible bunny, so I proceeded to do the same thing. Again, as I went back to my chair he pointed to a third unseeable furry critter with long ears and a cotton tail (so he said). As I approached this third imaginary rabbit and started to grab it by its airy ears, I suddenly stopped and thought, as I bent down, "Just who really needs help here?"

From the experience I came to realize and appreciate anew that if counseling is going to be beneficial, it must be based in reality. I gave up doing for clients what I thought they expected and learned to confront. I probably would have eventually learned to do these and other necessary helping techniques in counseling, but my client experience sped up the process. It helped me know that there was much I needed to do if I was not going to get lost in the history of being an outdated counselor in a postmodern world.

chapter 26

Testing a Theory: The Sound of Silence

*I*n my counseling program, I thought I learned one theory well: person-centered. Its origin was in the writings of the theorist Carl Rogers. I thought it had a lot of merit, and as a novice counselor, I imagined it would be easy to implement. The major part of it seemed to me to be reflection. If I could reflect well enough, I thought my clients would get better sooner because they would be able to hear their thoughts and feelings and become more congruent.

If some reflection was good, would not more be better? Thus one day I resolved to "out-Roger" Carl Rogers and become the most reflective counselor east of the Mississippi River. By nightfall, I thought, a number of clients would be much better off because of my stance. At 10 a.m. came the perfect opportunity to initiate my beliefs, for at that hour not only did I have my first appointment for the day but it was with a teenage girl.

"Who likes to talk more than teenage girls?" I wondered. "This young woman will naturally talk," I thought, "and as I reflect she will become more insightful into herself and begin to make choices and changes."

Unfortunately for me, the young woman who came to my office that day was as silent as light. She had been referred (i.e., mandated) to get counseling, and she did not want to see me or anybody else. Nevertheless, I put forth my best Rogerian style. I empathized with her situation and told her I was there to listen and reflect with her. She was not impressed. Instead of talking, she sat. I sat with her, hoping to reflect being open, interested, and respectful. None of it worked. The harder I tried, the more trying it was. Finally, after about 15 minutes of silence, which seemed like an eternity, I asked her if she had anything to say since she had been mute for most of our time together.

"Yes," was her reply. "I want to go now."

"Out the door?"

"Precisely."

Then she left, and the only thing I felt was the breeze from her passing by my chair and a strange emptiness inside. I had failed. I had been more like Roy Rogers than Carl Rogers. The result was that nothing happened.

After that time, I focused more on being myself. I did not forget theories. In fact, I tried to learn them better. I used them as models and adapted them in line with published research. My counseling became much improved.

chapter 27

Chipmunk Cheeks

I should probably have been tipped off initially by the way her cheeks bulged like a chipmunk's in late fall. I had frequently seen these cute, brown-furred, white-striped rodents carrying food in the pouches of their mouths on October afternoons. However, even though I was aware that my client had bulging cheeks, I pretended to be nonchalant as if all of the people I saw looked like her.

After all, I was working in a rural mental health center and I was used to seeing "interesting" people enter the front door with sometimes rather "unusual" stories, problems, and even facial expressions. So, rather than say anything that might call into question the physical looks of my new client, I simply introduced myself and asked her to follow me up to my second-floor office for counseling.

She complied in silence. The fact that she did not appear talkative did not concern me. A lot of new clients were not very communicative. They were often timid, especially at first, and wondered what to do, when, and how. Therefore, I tried to treat my client with the utmost respect, realizing that was the best way to establish rapport and get the process of therapy started.

When we entered my office, I invited her to take a chair next to mine. She complied a second time quite quietly and I thought, "This session should go well." That thought lasted for all of 30 seconds for as I looked at her, I noticed she was moving material around in her mouth. To put it in a straightforward, no-nonsense way—she was chewing something!

"Oh," I reflected in my mind, "she must have visited a fast food restaurant right before she arrived. I'll bet she is just finishing up her hamburger or French fries."

Fortunately for me I am not a gambler, for there is little more that could have been further from the truth.

Asking a closed-ended, informational question, I inquired, "Did you just go to McDonald's?"

She shook her head from side to side politely as if she was not sure why I would ask such a question.

Realizing I had no idea as to what to ask next, I said, "Well, let's get started." With those words out, the corners of her mouth curled upward and my optimism about a good first session returned—for all of about 2 seconds. My client was still speechless. Somehow in the midst of this seemingly strange behavior, I knew that the "Sound of Silence," once a great hit song by Simon and Garfunkel, would not be playing in our session.

Still, I persevered. I had had rougher beginnings and all had turned out all right. "A direct approach is what is needed," I surmised, and I know just what to do. Thus, with all my directness and discomfort in being a reflective Rogerian acting like a behavioral Skinnerian, I probed with the never failing, always-on-target inquiry of "What brings you here?"

My client now looked a little more uncomfortable. She was a bit pale and I noticed that the modest chewing motion she had made when I first saw her was accelerating.

"Whoa!" is all I could mutter under my breath. "Have I struck a nerve here or what?"

Thus, I countered with an empathetic, almost sympathetic coaxing, saying, "You know, Mrs. Jones, you do not have to tell me anything. Counseling is a process where you are free to act and interact as suits you best."

I expected she would calm down and relax with that assurance but instead she seemed more pensive as she looked around the room as if she were seeking a sign of comfort. "I could have been an engineer" flashed through my mind instantaneously but just as quickly disappeared, for I realized something was wrong.

And then I noticed that she was pointing. "They did not tell me my client was mute," I sighed under my breath. "However, I can handle mutes, selective or not. It just requires a little more energy." Thus, I sat up on the edge of my chair to respond to the challenge.

"I am not sure what you are trying to convey," I told her. "Point or give me a signal that shows me what you wish to let me know."

With that permission, she scrunched her face up like a witch on Halloween, and let her somewhat unkempt black hair flow over her shoulders in a fluid motion.

"Hag!" I yelled out impulsively, realizing as I did that if the word escaped the confines of my office or if we were not playing charades, I could be in a lot of trouble.

However, to my relief she gave me a sign, like the letter "B" which I added to the word I had just vocalized. After I dropped the "H," I shouted in an excited voice "Bag! You want a bag! You want a bag!"

But ... and I should never have even raised the question, "Why do you want a bag?"

With that query, my what-I-thought-until-then was a mute, middle-aged woman seeking my assistance started jumping up and down. As she did she seemed to be chewing more furiously than ever and making the motion of a curvy letter with her hands.

"She's having a fit" was the first thought that came into my mind.

The second was "She's jumping so hard the staff on the first floor will hear her and come investigate."

My third thought was "I'm going to lose my license. I just called this woman a 'hag' and I do not think 'bounce therapy' is in any book on appropriate helping theories."

Then it struck me. The word "fit," the heavy chewing, and the sign of the letter "S" being made with her hands suddenly made sense.

"She's got to spit! That's why she needs the bag!" It was like saying mentally, "There she blows!" And just as quickly as that insight entered my mind, I must confess that another word beginning with the letter "S" and having to do with elimination followed.

"Holy Moly!" I said silently. "How am I going to handle this situation? I do not keep plastic bags in my office for clients to spit in."

But just when panic was about to materialize, I saw a way out—the window! I raced to it as fast as possible, raised it as high as it would go, and although I was tempted to jump, I instead waved my bouncy, chewy, beginning-to-be-all-gooey client over to the open air, helped her lean out, and gave her an encouraging and firm slap on the back.

Out flew a wad of tobacco that I estimated to be about the size of Texas, along with some extra fine brownish juice that could have filled a catfish pond. All of it sailed through the air like an asteroid from outer space with a fluid tail. Finally it landed with a thud and a splash at the foot of an old, orange-leafed maple tree about 10 feet away. The sight was not particularly appealing and I thought I might need a bag for a different reason than my client had. Thankfully, my stomach quickly settled down.

As this incident ended, my client pulled her head back in, wiped her mouth with her sweatshirt sleeve (that was brown), and seemed to be as relieved as I was that the little adventure we had just been through was finished. Her addiction to chewing tobacco had taken a toll on us both.

She had been unable to tell me her needs and I had been unable to tell what she needed.

With a smile she apologized and sheepishly, so did I. The words were less frantic now. Nothing like "hag" came out. Instead, nice-sounding thoughts and feelings began to flow. Her cheeks were much less puffy. They almost looked hollow. The session that had started so badly thus proceeded to end positively.

The only down side of the incident (besides its absurdity and franticness) was the lasting impact it had on my appetite. Even now when I order pancakes or waffles, I always eat them plain. But while maple syrup is not on my menu, nonverbal behavior is. I am ever vigilant in observing it in my clients.

Note. From Goldin, E., Bordan, T., Araoz, D. L., Gladding, S. T., Kaplan, D., Krumboltz, J., & Lazarus, A. (2006). Humor in counseling: Leader perspectives. *Journal of Counseling & Development, 84,* 397–405.

chapter 28

The Right to Struggle

*L*ife is challenging and often unpredictable. Starting at an early age, we are inundated with numerous choices in almost everything we do. That fact came home to me a few months ago as I was saying "good night" to my son, Tim. As we were parting he started a conversation with me about a decision that lay before him. I was honored that he sought me out and for about 45 minutes, we talked in a quiet but serious way. As the discussion came to a close, he looked at me and said, "You know, Dad, you're a lousy counselor."

Taken somewhat aback, I asked, "What do you mean?"

To which Tim replied, "We've talked for a long time and yet you haven't given me any advice."

As I reflected, I realized that Tim was correct. Measured by the standards that he had in his mind and those of many dictionaries, I had not lived up to the definition that a counselor is one who offers advice. Yet my belief is that a counselor (and a parent) is one who empowers. Giving advice seldom strengthens a person. Think about it. What advice have you received that was especially helpful?

"Buy low, sell high." "Be yourself." "Be polite." "Don't cry over spilled milk." "Always wear clean underwear in case you are in an accident." "Count to 10 when you get angry." "Sit up straight."

The trouble with advice is that it is often filled with platitudes and common sense, except maybe the suggestion to wear clean underwear in case of an accident. However, other difficulties with advice are more serious. Advice, especially from an authority figure, such as a counselor, is between unequals. The person less powerful may feel obligated to accept and comply with the advice. When such is the case, the recipient is prevented from struggling with the complexities of a situation or a decision and thus comes to a premature closure. As a result, the receiver becomes weaker instead of stronger because options have simply been cut off. In addition, the person will have lost an opportunity for reflection and the experience of working through ambiguity surrounding an interpersonal or growth-enhancing relationship. Furthermore, if the advice is wrong there is often no way to rectify the matter. Therefore, instead of helping someone build life skills, advice in counseling fosters dependency, desperation, and depression so that an individual begins to be less reliant on and less congruent with himself or herself.

The extreme of advice—dependence—showed up on my doorstep a number of years ago when one of my clients literally followed me home.

"Don," I began, "our session at the mental health center ended an hour ago. I do not understand why you are sitting in front of my apartment door."

Don did not blink but rather stated, "I need to know how to handle my mother. What should I do? You didn't tell me during our meeting."

He was right. I had not told Don exactly what to do. However, in our next session, I revisited the exploration I had done with Don initially on what he was doing and what he wanted to do. He left that session, unlike the first, with an understanding of options that he generated. The point is that in being a counselor it is crucial to be with our clients as they wrestle with concerns, issues, and ideas. That can be done when we use our theoretical and clinical skills to foster their development in ways that allow them to grow as independent decision-makers.

While all of these comments may seem obvious, they are not. Too many times, people in helping professions want to please or be powerful. By taking either stance they become like a beauty contestant. While it might be nice to be admired, revered, or considered "most congenial," none of those qualities is important for its own sake in counseling. Rather, it is essential that we within the profession constantly ask ourselves both what we are doing and its intended outcome. Through self-examination, peer consultation, and supervision, we can avoid slipping into advice giving. By so doing, those we serve, like my son or former client, may not initially be pleased with our responses. However, in the long run, they will benefit, for in the process of struggling they will have gained a sense of themselves and their power that no advisor or advice can impart. Though not guaranteed by the Constitution, the right to struggle is life-giving and gives value and meaning to our lives.

Note. From Gladding, S. T. (2005b, February). The right to struggle. *Counseling Today*, p. 5.

chapter | 29

Be Modest

eople who seek counseling do so for many reasons. Some believe you can help them sort out their personal and career concerns, and they are usually right. Others, however, believe you can work miracles such as making them motivated, insightful, and successful. They are usually sincere in these beliefs, but wrong. Before I became a counselor, I found out the importance of modesty and its impact on expectations.

I was in divinity school at the time. I had broken my ankle in an intramural game of volleyball in December, so instead of driving back to school I took a plane after the semester break. The first leg of the trip went well as I flew from my home in Atlanta to New York City aboard a spacious jet. However, the second leg of my trip was much harder. My flight from New York to New Haven, Connecticut, where I was studying, was aboard a single-engine plane with three seats. The pilot had one, I had the other, and a heavyset woman easily occupied the rest of the remaining space. The woman was pleasant, and we soon established rapport and struck up a conversation. In the middle of our talk she asked me what I was currently doing, and I made the mistake of telling her with some enthusiasm and probably a bit of pride that I was studying theology.

Then it happened! Over the Long Island Sound, the engine suddenly quit. It went dead, and all we could hear around us was the silence of air as we glided along briefly for a moment in the eerie pretense that nothing was wrong. Yet in that instant, I looked at my fellow passenger and she at me. Then, reaching out with two meaty hands, she grabbed me by my tie, pulled me up to her face, and with a brief but forceful breath she uttered just one word, "Pray."

I wanted to tell her that I could not breathe, let alone pray. I also wanted to thank her for choking me to death so I would not drown. Yet, before I could do any of these things, the engine started again, and she dropped me to the floor like a stone. With the release, I regained my composure, said a little prayer of thanks, moved as far away from the woman as I could, and vowed to always be modest from then on in how I presented myself and what I did.

Since that time, I have found that if expectations of clients in regard to who you are and what you can do are not too high, they are usually better off and so are you.

chapter 30

A Door, a Phone, a Window

I grew up trusting people, and that attitude toward others spilled over into counseling. However, it might have been better for me initially had it not been so. The reason is the way I arranged the first office I did not share with others. The office was an elongated room with cinder brick walls. Because of its shape, I had to place my desk and chairs in less than ideal ways in order to make best use of the space. In the process I placed the desk at the front of the room near the door with the phone on it, placed my clients' chairs next, and finally put my chair closest to the window.

"I'll enjoy the view and the fresh air more if I sit here," I thought.

And so I did for several months. However, as fate would have it, one day I was asked to see a very disturbed client for an evaluation. I could tell on encountering him that the task was not going to be easy. Nevertheless, I asked him to follow me to my office. On arriving I motioned for him to sit where my clients usually did. I, in turn, took my seat. About 2 minutes later, I realized I was in trouble. The disheveled man was becoming agitated and hostile. He was verbally threatening and was big enough to be physically intimidating.

I needed help, but the client was between me, the door, and the phone. I had a problem. I tried everything I knew to calm him and the situation, but things steadily grew worse. There was no way to finesse my way past the client, and he was moving in the wrong direction, toward me. Thus, I headed toward the window. It was unlocked and opened easily. I was out of it in the twinkling of an eye and not a second too soon. It was a relief when I hit the ground, but I did not stop to congratulate myself for surviving the drop of about 4 feet. Instead, I went to get help and entered the front of the building where I greeted our surprised receptionist.

"I thought you were in with a client," she said.

"I was," I replied, "but I had to leave." Then I quickly explained to her what was happening and she went to the phone to do her duty. Soon the emergency medical personnel arrived and my client was calmed.

Although I was a bit embarrassed about being a counselor dropout that day, I went to school on the experience. The next morning, the phone on the desk came closer to my chair and within easy reach should an emergency arise. My chair moved too and became situated between my client and the door. The window remained where it was.

chapter 31

The Price of Being Ill Prepared

*W*hen I did my initial graduate school work at Yale, one day I went out for a ride with a friend. We went along an unmarked route in the rolling hill country of western Connecticut and had a wonderful time exploring the Nutmeg State. However, as we attempted to return at dusk, we made one wrong turn after another as we tried to figure out (without a map) where we were and how we would get back to our residence hall.

As if we were not suffering enough for our folly of being ill prepared, my friend made an illegal turn across a busy highway in front of a Connecticut State Highway Patrol car. Needless to say, the sharp eyes of the trooper in the car spotted us. Soon we had been pulled over with the state trooper on the driver's side of the car talking to my friend.

"You can't make a left turn like that," the trooper said.

To which my friend replied, "That's not true. I just did."

My friend was correct. He knew what he had done, and he wanted to assure the officer that it was possible. Unfortunately, the possible was also illegal and had a fine attached to it. Some hours later when we finally reached our destination, my friend said in summing up our day, "Getting lost costs a lot."

Likewise in counseling, there is a high price associated with poor preparation or illegal or unethical behavior. Such action takes us and our clients down the wrong roads or in the wrong directions. The result is that time, energy, resources, abilities, and hope are wasted and can never be recovered.

chapter 32

The Wrong Side of Presentations

art of one's professional responsibility is to attend and make presentations on clinical aspects of counseling. It is much easier to attend than to present.

In order to present, you not only have to formulate ideas but also develop them in such a way that others find your words interesting, informative, and ultimately educational. There are several ways I have found that produce certain failure.

First, if you do not want people coming back to ever hear you again, become a part of a large, uncoordinated group that merely lectures to those in attendance. I did this once and only once. I was part of a panel at an American Counseling Association convention. Each of the presenters was a notable and quotable type of person, but we had not rehearsed. When the program was over, a young man came up to me and said, "Who was responsible for this program?"

Being modest I replied, "Well, all of us really, but I organized it."

"It was awful," he said. "You guys need to get your act together." With that, he walked away, and I woke up to the reality that he was right.

The second way not to be successful as a presenter is to find out as little as you can about your audience. I again made such a mistake at a large university gathering where I was making a presentation on groups. Instead of finding out what participants knew about the subject, who they were, or what their interests were, I plunged right in with my prepared remarks. No one fell out of a chair into the aisle in a dead faint or started foaming at the mouth, but the presentation was less than a success. No one was connected with each other or me. Thus, the words I spoke lost their relevance and potency.

A final guideline for being unsuccessful in presenting is to stay completely cognitive and talk in a monotone. I am not a monotone type of guy as a rule, but I confess to once being completely so at a state counseling convention. I did not stray from my prepared remarks. However, my audience strayed mentally (and some physically) from the room. The sound of hard syllables crashing together can be deafening and demoralizing.

As I said initially, it is easier to attend than present at a conference. But presentations have multiple payoffs in the ways they stimulate thinking and lead to the discovery of new knowledge and friendships. The secret of such outcomes, however, is being well prepared and preparing audiences as well. An old rock-and-roll group used to be called the Monotones, but it is not a name we want to be called as counselors, especially during presentations.

chapter 33

Learning the Lingo

art of being an effective counselor involves understanding, not just hearing, a client's words. Otherwise, all kinds of mischief may occur.

The importance of understanding language was initially called to my attention when I was a graduate student at Yale. On the first morning of class, a friend from New Jersey said to me, "Let's go get a Danish."

Taken aback, I replied, "Can we and why would we want to?" (I had no desire to intentionally go after someone from Scandinavia.)

He was as surprised by my remark as I was by his. However, he insisted, and before you could say "sugar topping" we stood in front of a pastry shop in downtown New Haven.

"So what kind of Danish do you want?" he said as we gazed at the goodies in the window.

"I don't see any Danish," I replied.

"Well," a bit exasperated, he said, "what do you call those things right in front of your eyes?"

"Sweet rolls," I responded (for that is what they were called in my native state of Georgia).

"Oh," was all he could say. "Here we call them Danish." Then we walked into the shop with a better understanding of each other and the power of words.

In counseling, two similar situations concerning language stand out in my memory. In one, my client kept talking about "busting" the soil. What he meant was he needed to plow. In the second (I'm embarrassed to say), a teenage girl I was counseling mentioned that the night before she had "smoked a roach" and that it nearly drove her crazy.

"I can imagine it would," I remember saying. "Roaches are not clean insects."

Only after she stopped laughing did I realize she had not lit up a brown creepy creature that is the scourge of people everywhere. Instead, she had inhaled the last drags of a marijuana cigarette.

Listening is only as powerful as one's ability to understand.

chapter 34

The Wake-Up Dream

My initial experience on the importance of interaction in learning came as a result of a class I taught in which I was an adjunct instructor. The course was an introduction to psychology that met at 8 a.m. at a local community college. I worked hard on the course because I hoped to someday become a professor. However, the class schedule was against me because I did not believe in life before 10 a.m. (and my students apparently did not either).

My limited knowledge of the subject was also a drawback. And to make matters worse, my method of delivery was disastrous. I lectured every day with all the pizzazz of a drone bee in autumn. I realized after about the fifth class session that I was boring my students, but I continued to hope they would finally find the material and me interesting. Alas, it did not happen.

Then one night after working on my notes into the wee hours, I fell asleep and had a dream. In it, I saw my students lining up in front of my desk, with me standing on top of the desk behind a lectern. Like ducks in a carnival shooting gallery, each student came by and would tilt his or her head backward. I would grab a sheet of lecture material, place it over his or her mouth, and with a cannon ramrod that was close by, stuff the material down the student's gullet. It was a scene full of pressure, frustration, and absurdity.

The intensity of the dream woke me up. In my awareness of the moment I knew I had a choice. I could continue as I was and the class atmosphere would degenerate, or I could try something (almost anything) new. I opted for the latter. The next day I had the class circle up in a group and began by sharing the dream with them. That was the start of our first group discussion. It was a satisfying and sensitive experience for us all. It would never have happened if I had dismissed the awareness of the dream and called it a nightmare. Instead, I gave up an old way of working and tried something new. The interactive nature of the working relationship that resulted with the class was worth making.

chapter 35

Love on an Academic Level

*I*t was February 14th and I had taken a late flight from my home in North Carolina to Colorado. When I arrived at my destination in Colorado Springs, I was confused. I thought I was to be met by someone from the publishing company on whose editorial board I served. Seeing no one, I waited and took in my surroundings. The airport was unfamiliar to me but finally I saw a sign of hope. It read "Information."

With a sense of hope, I made my way over to a booth where a young woman stood with a red rose pinned to her lapel.

"Excuse me," I said. "I am here for Love."

She looked me up and down in a respectful but skeptical way. Then with a tinge of sarcasm in her voice she replied, "I'll just bet you are!"

Startled at first, I continued, "Someone was to meet me here, I thought."

"Maybe you should think again," she answered. "Sometimes they just don't show, cowboy. That's Valentine's Day for you."

Then it struck me. She thought I was seeking love as in amore, affection, passion, and pleasure. She assumed when I said "love" that I was talking about that tinkling, tingling, wonderfully exciting, head-over-heels, inviting emotion felt between two people who have become deeply and emotionally engrossed with one another.

"Oh no," I countered in a somewhat embarrassed way. "You see, I'm not here for that kind of love."

She blinked, backed off a few steps as if I might have a highly contagious disease, and somewhat hesitantly asked, "Then what kind of love are you seeking?"

Publishing Love. Stan Love. The Love that comes printed on paper in books and monographs. It is not always goose bump exciting but the products that Mr. Love delivers last longer than most romances.

"Do you know what I'm talking about?" I questioned.

"I haven't a clue," she confessed, "but I hope you find love wherever it or he, or maybe even she, may be."

With those words our conversation ended and I called a taxi to take me to Love Publishing Company.

In looking back on that Valentine's Day and my memorable, if less than romantic, conversation, I am reminded of the importance of levity and the lessons we learn from it. Often levity is the lever that helps us move from seeing life as a tragedy to experiencing life as a comedy. That perspective makes life with others not only bearable, but fulfilling and even fun.

The Spanish Inquisition or How Not to Write a Resume

The Spanish Inquisition is an infamous event. It defined a period and the people in it in a way that has connotations to this day. It will always be a marker event in history.

So why mention the Spanish Inquisition when the emphasis here is on writing a resume? Simple. I took five years of Spanish—two in high school and three in college. Yet, on one of the first resumes I ever sent out for a job, I misspelled the word *Spanish*. Amazingly, I was called in for an interview as a finalist for the position for which I had applied. I was hopeful that my mistake might go unnoticed. However, after the initial warm greetings one of the committee members interviewing me pointed out the error.

"Ouch," I thought. "Caught! There is no escape."

If the slip-up had just been noted and quoted, I think I would have been okay. But such was not the case. The committee member pressed me on how I could have been so careless. Would I show the same kind of behavior at the institution that was considering hiring me? Did I have a nonchalant manner by nature? If the committee member were to visit my office would he see a chaotic display of books, papers, and red-leaded pencils thrown around as if they were worthless? The questions went on from there and came fast and furious.

At first I tried to field them diplomatically and accurately. However, after about the fifth question, I realized that my efforts were not going to be well received. My questioner was out to make a point or two that had little to do with my mistake. Apparently, he was upset with what he considered to be the sloppy nature of his colleagues and he wanted them to know it.

Nevertheless, I have taken the memory of that day to heart. I think neatness, except in mud wrestling or pig farming, is crucial to success. We are judged by our ability to seem competent in the midst of chaos. First impressions last, and last impressions are the first things most people remember about us. Thus, 30 years from the event, I read carefully almost everything I write. I only depend on computer programs, such as Spell Check, up to a point. I am particularly sensitive to words I know by heart. To err is human, but I do not want to be too human too often... especially in my professional life.

Points to Ponder

1. When have you failed in something you tried? What did you learn from it? How have you changed since then?

2. In your studies or travels, have you ever been ill prepared? What happened? What did you do differently after that?

3. What words or descriptive terms have you learned in recent years? How did this new language help you better understand yourself and your environment?

SKILLS AND PROCESSES

She works in a world I have never known
full of rainbow pills and lilac candles
woven together with simple time-stitches
a pattern of color in a gray fabric factory
where she spends her days spinning threads
that go to Chicago by night.
Once with a little girl smile and a giggle
she flew to Atlanta in her mind,
opening the door to instant adventure
far from her present fatigue.
That was a journey we shared
arranging her thoughts in patchwork patterns
until the designs and desires came together.

—Gladding, 1974[4]

*A*s counselors we bring special knowledge and skills into our interactions with others. We are aware of human growth and development as well as clinical pathology. We are also informed as to what skills work best with which clients and when. Therefore, when we are working with clients, part of our focus is on the processes we will use to help them get beyond the places where they are stuck so that they do not get dysfunctional or remain sick, but rather grow.

In the vignettes in this section, the focus is on skills and processes that lead us as people and professionals to make needed choices and changes in regard to what we are doing. It is crucial, as the story "Afraid of Blood" implies, that we make sure we help clients keep their lives and actions in perspective even when they are getting better. Skills and processes are tools, and we as counselors must use them carefully.

chapter 37

The Basics

*I*n counseling, the basics are important. This fact came home to me one day in an experience with my oldest son, Ben, when he was 3-years old. At that time, we had moved into a new house with a banister on the second-floor landing. One morning soon after the move, Ben put his head through the banister railings and began to cry as he struggled to get free. His cries brought his mother to the rescue. She pulled, pushed, greased his head with oil, and did all within her power to help him escape his entrapment. But alas, her efforts were in vain.

Finally, as my wife was about to cut the banister railings, she said in exasperation, "How did you ever get yourself caught like this?"

The boy's reply was to raise his head up and wiggle his body through the rails back to the landing so that he was free once more. "Like this," he said, as he retraced his steps. To his surprise and to the delight of his mother, he had helped himself by remembering the basics of how he got to where he was in the first place.

As counselors we depend on basic knowledge and skills. Part of that knowledge is remembering not to do a client's work for him or her, and to stay cognizant of where we have been in our sessions as well as where we are going.

chapter 38

The Difficulty of Change

C hange is a critical element in counseling, but it does not always come easy. We are creatures of habit, and once a routine is established, the pattern—even if it is dysfunctional—is hard to break. For example, people in abusive situations often tend to stay in them rather than leave because they prefer a known environment and a predictable pattern of behavior to what is unknown. The difficulty of change has been one I have seen throughout my career, but it was initially demonstrated to me, at least on a mechanical level, when I was a somewhat financially strapped and struggling graduate student.

I needed to make a local telephone call. The cost for such calls then was a dime. I had a quarter. Thus, as I picked up the receiver in the telephone booth, I wondered if I would receive change back if I deposited my coin. I did not have to ponder the question long. Above the phone were information and instructions from the company. One sentence near the end of this material read, "This phone does not give change."

Under the sentence was one scrawled in black ink from a disgruntled customer, I am sure, that read, "It doesn't even try!"

So I found out, on that day at least, that my wishes for change were not going to be fulfilled. Therefore, I talked for as long as I could on the call to hopefully get my money's worth and then some. However, the more important lesson that I took from the experience and that I have since applied to counseling is that some people are more like the telephone I called from than others. Those who do not try do not change, despite our wishes or skills.

chapter 39

The Pace of Change

When my children were young, they used to enjoy gathering their loose change and wrapping similar coins together. The process was educational and fun. It even became ritualized at one time into a family affair, and Fridays became "wrap nights." After our wrapping, I would take the rolls of coins to the campus bank on Mondays to make an exchange and bring back dollar bills in return.

One time, however, this ordeal got a bit out of hand. The children had saved up more than usual, and instead of several rolls of coins, I ended up carrying $56 worth of silver and copper (mostly pennies) onto campus one day. My coat and pants pockets were stuffed. To make matters worse, I could not find a parking space near the campus bank. As fate would have it on that hot summer morning, I got out of my car filled with determination but loaded down with heavy metal. After a few steps, I felt myself wobble. The task was more than I had envisioned. My movement became slower, and my knees began to buckle just slightly as I bent toward the ground like a tree during a windstorm. Still I continued with a swaying motion.

However, just as the bank entered my sight so did an important university official. Because I was not moving fast and was slouched over, he quickly overtook me, and with a worried look on his face, he said, "Sam, what's wrong?"

Not wanting him to think I was being frivolous in regard to my regular duties and yet not wanting to be less than truthful about the coins I was carrying, I replied,

"I think I've just become overwhelmed by change."

Indeed, I had. I was trying to carry too much. Instead of being engaged in a fun process, I was now struggling to just keep going. The same is true with change for clients and colleagues. They usually do best when they (and we) do not try to do everything at the same time. Small change is manageable. Too much change all at once can be debilitating.

chapter 40

Boundaries: An Awakening

*I*t was 2 a.m. when the phone rang. I had been asleep for approximately three hours. Therefore, I was not quite sure whether the ringing I heard was from a dream within my head or from an outside stimulus. However, in a somewhat groggy manner, I answered the phone and muttered "Hello."

"Dr. Gladding," a perky female voice on the other end sang out, "this is Jane. Remember me? I'm one of your clients."

"Yes."

"Well," she continued, "I know it is 2 a.m., but I just can't get to sleep tonight." Her voice was almost cheerful.

"Jane, what have you tried doing to get to sleep?"

"Nothing," she said somewhat gleefully. "I'm just not sleeping so I thought I'd call you and talk."

"Jane, I don't know if this will shock you, but I can sleep. In fact, just now I was sleeping quite well. I would suggest you try to get some sleep. If you can't, please call the emergency number I gave you. If you want to call the office tomorrow, I am sure we can arrange an appointment soon." With that, I hung up, rolled over, and went back to sleep.

The next morning Jane arranged an appointment and came to see me. After that time, she no longer called me late at night or at home. Although my behavior may have initially seemed to her to be rude, it set a boundary regarding our relationship.

Most boundaries can and should be set through using a professional disclosure statement during the first session of counseling. If boundaries are not set, clients can become intrusive and inappropriately interrupt your private life. When that happens, you as a counselor will lose more than sleep, and no one will be helped in the long run.

chapter 41

Modeling: A Case of Starlings

"I'm afraid of starlings," she said. "They swoop down so low and so fast that I am fearful they will peck me on the head or fly into my face and I will be injured."

I sat there nodding, my head shaking up and down, while my mind was trying to comprehend what my client was talking about. So I responded with an investigative comment. "Tell me more."

"Well, I don't know exactly anything else to say. I'm just scared, and since I live on a farm, I am finding my life unpleasant. I'm afraid to walk outside to the barn."

"Has anyone you know had a starling peck them on the head or fly into their face?"

"No."

"Are there a lot of incidents that you've read about where people were hurt by starlings?"

Once again the answer was negative.

However, the facts were not sufficient. My client was still fearful. I could see it in her eyes and hear it in her voice. I was not going to talk her out of her fear.

"How far away from here is your farm?"

"About a 15-minute drive," she said.

"Well, how about if we go for a visit now and see these starlings?"

"Okay," she responded, and we were out the door and into her car as quickly as a bird on the wing.

When we reached the farm, we initially stayed in the car as she pointed the birds out to me.

"Let's go for a walk," I suggested in my best invitational voice.

She shook her head from side to side.

"Okay," I said. "I'll go walk and you watch."

I did and she did.

Sure enough, the starlings swooped down low near my head like dive-bombers in a World War II movie. They came in swiftly, but they seemed to have a sense of space and place. They came close but never really came that near to where I felt I had to fear for my safety. The first day ended with my client watching.

However, the next session, which was held at the farm again, was one in which she participated after seeing me walk around the barn once by myself. She joined me, and as we strolled we talked about the nature of starlings swooping down to get insects stirred up by people or animals. She was still scared but less so than before.

Later sessions were spent in similar ways with me videotaping her and showing her how the birds reacted to her. She then started studying herself as much as she did the birds' movements. The result was an action she called the "bird walk" where she showed me how she could move in such a way that she was comfortable with herself in the presence of starlings.

It was through seeing that she came into believing that she need not be afraid of starlings. Counseling is sometimes a profession of demonstrations. We need to model and often lead by example before we can expect any differences in our clients. Change does not come through reason, knowledge, or even insight alone. It is a process in which actions can, and often do, speak louder than words.

chapter 42

Mr. TBA: The Importance of Knowing Others

*T*he importance of establishing rapport in a relationship with others came when I was an instructor at a community college across the street from the mental health center where I worked. Because I was not asked to teach until a couple of days before the term began, the college had simply noted under "Introduction to Psychology" that the instructor would be named later and had done so with the traditional abbreviation "TBA" (to be announced). Well, as fate would have it, on the opening day of class one of my students was late. She came in about halfway through the class and quietly slid into a blue plastic desk chair in the only place left—at the front of the room. When I finished my remarks for the day and as the class was leaving, I caught the eye of the tardy student and asked her to see me for a minute so I could give her a syllabus. Being new to the college and having missed introductions, when she approached me she said, "I'm really sorry I was late, Mr. TBA. I had car trouble. By the way, what kind of name is TBA? Is it Italian? My ancestors were from Italy, you know."

Well, after she realized my name was not TBA and I was not Italian and she had her assignments for the term, she went away disappointed but aware of our relationship and how it would play out. Although this example is a bit silly, it illustrates, I hope, the importance of initial introductions and that establishing rapport with people is crucial to developing relationships with them both inside and outside of counseling. Rapport building is never based on assumptions alone or on printed facts.

chapter 43

Empathy

*E*mpathy, as Carl Rogers once said, is the ability to enter the private world of someone else and be thoroughly at home in it. It is a quality that makes a difference in whether our clients change or not.

When I first learned about empathy, I thought it would be a skill that would come naturally to counselors and those seeking to be counselors. I found out, however, that empathy is not always generously distributed among those who are in or who wish to enter counseling as a profession.

A student revealed this fact to me several years after I began teaching counselor education. She was a young woman who was articulate, bright, and full of energy. She was wonderful in many ways. Yet, she could not demonstrate an ability to master empathy beyond an elementary level. I have no doubt she felt for her clients. The trouble was she could not convey it. In frustration, she usually ended up offering clients advice rather than letting them know that she felt with them. Finally, one day after a particularly tough supervision session, she confessed her inadequacy in the domain of empathy to me by saying, "Feelings to me are just like music. When a song is over, I always play the next selection."

Her message spoke volumes (if not albums) about her ability and suitability for the counseling profession. She was kind and intelligent, but she lacked the patience to stay with a client and to deeply feel what the client might be experiencing.

We, as counselors, cannot truly be with or help others beyond the realm of giving information unless we can empathize with them. That is a challenge and requires not only that we suspend judgment, but also that we activate the right words within us like musicians playing the proper notes in a symphony or band. In such sound, there is connectivity that brings people together.

chapter 44

Afraid of Blood

She came to me is desperation. I knew she did not want to be there. Yet, there she was. Her intake form stated that she had a phobia. It was specific: blood.

I began our session by talking about phobias and the foundation for them. She was mildly interested but finally stopped me in mid-sentence and with some emotion said, "I've got to get over this fear fast."

"What's the rush?" I inquired.

"I want to go to medical school. A physician can't be afraid of blood."

She was right. Medicine of even the gentlest nature deals with blood. So, I suggested we center our sessions on Joseph Wolpe's systematic desensitization approach and go from there. She readily agreed once she understood the process, and within a few sessions she had gone through her hierarchy of most feared situations involving blood.

"What do I do next?" she asked.

"I don't think you have to do much more of anything, but if you wish you could view some movies that are of minor operations," I offered. She did and viewed some with major operations, too.

Then her question came again: "What do I do next?"

"Nothing," I said. "I think you have done enough and you have completely overcome your problem."

However, she did not quit, and the last time I saw her she had just come back from a visit to a slaughterhouse.

Sometimes what is therapeutic can be taken to extremes. Knowing how far to take a process and when to stop is crucial. Preventive measures can be therapeutic, but if overdone or taken to extremes they can lead to disorders.

chapter 45

Omelets

A client theme I have heard constantly over the years is that of regret. "If only I had not said what I said or did what I did, everything would be so much better." Yet, people make mistakes and many times do not forgive themselves—let alone forget such incidents.

The importance of working in the "now" in such cases became apparent to me one day when I was seeing a man who was upset about the course of his life. He had had a bad relationship with his parents, he had chosen an inappropriate college and an esoteric major, he had married the wrong woman twice, and his career track had been as spotty as a leopard. So at the age of 56, he said, "I want to go back and do it all over again."

"That would be nice," I replied, "but can you?"

He sighed and looked down at the ground. I could read his disappointment in my response. I did not want him to be unrealistic about his life as it was now. However, I did not want him to become hopelessly depressed over the state of his existence either. So I said, knowing a little about his personal habits, "Paul, what do you usually have for breakfast?"

"Why, a fried egg," he said.

"And if you make a mistake in breaking the egg, what do you do?"

"Well, either I break another and make an omelet or I scramble the egg."

"But you don't try to put the egg back in its casing?"

He laughed. "That would be impossible."

And then he caught the implication of what he knew to be true. He could not undo what had been done, but he could take the mess that lay before him and try to make the most of it by learning from it and forming it into something that was more palatable physically and mentally than what he had now.

People cannot unscramble eggs or undo events. But making the most out of what has been rather than trying to do the impossible can make a big difference in how one grows and lives.

chapter 46

The Concrete Counselor

When my two oldest sons turned 18, they received, aside from family gifts, a couple of other "presents." One was a free razor from Gillette. The other was a letter from the Selective Service Administration reminding them to register for the draft. Both of these bequests were tangible reminders that they had reached a milestone in life.

In counseling, the material prompts of passing time and growth are not so apparent. We often do not know if the individuals, groups, or families with whom we work have made significant changes. The reason is that transitions are time-sensitive. People make them when they are ready and able. Sometimes we catch people at opportune times. They are frustrated, discouraged, or emotionally elevated to the point that they will try almost anything different. That is when and where our skills come into play in altruistic and productive ways.

However, such is not the case for every client. We have all had those moments when we questioned why someone came to see us or if we chose the right intervention. It is during those frustratingly reflective times that we wonder whether we should have been more concrete or direct.

Yet, while concreteness has a place in counseling, this profession is not for those who have a need to see immediate results. It is more subtle. We as counselors live on the edge of the unseen. It is not an easy place to dwell. Unlike those in construction, on many days we cannot overtly witness what we have accomplished. That is why patience, faith, and process are so important in our lives. There are also two other qualities that are essential: a knowledge of development and creativity.

Since its inception, counseling has embraced development as one of its underpinnings. Development may be discontinuous and sudden. More often, development is continuous and gradual. Some of our more knowledgeable professionals have written about the importance of development in life and its significance in counseling. I particularly like the writings of Ken West on this subject. Allen and Mary Ivey also have incorporated development, especially Jean Piaget's work, into their developmental counseling theory.

Likewise, creativity plays a prominent role in what we do as counselors and how we help clients move to new levels. As counselors, we are co-creators with clients in their march towards more maturity, better health, and a happier life. Thelma Duffey and the Association for Creativity in Counseling represent the best of this acknowledgment of the power of creativity in counseling. We must always be research-based as a profession, but we must also be aware that those who have led us best, longest, and strongest have been people whose courage and sense of adventure allowed them to do different things in distinct ways. Whether we are in leadership or "in the trenches," we should not forget that being creative in counseling is doing something novel that is practical and useful.

So, in counseling we must remember that while concreteness is crucial to the outcome of housing and highways, it may not always be what we attain when working with clients. Therefore, we must think developmentally and creatively if we are not to be discouraged, discontent, and dismissive. One other thing to keep in mind is balance. Counseling is multifaceted. It consists of a wide range of topics and populations. Its settings range from educational institutions to clinics. It encompasses wellness, prevention, and treatment. Practitioners come from many cultures and have multiple and diverse beliefs and backgrounds. Research and practice go together. Therefore, as professionals we can never wed ourselves to one agenda or a single way of working lest we become like a one-trick pony whose act and activity becomes mundane and insignificant.

Concreteness is essential in some services and circles. But skills based on research, combined with patience, process, a developmental perspective, and creativity, will take us much farther as counselors in helping our clients change and grow.

Points to Ponder

1. What memorable changes have you made in life? Do you think small or big changes are easiest to implement? Why?

2. What behaviors have you or those you know modeled well? What were the results?

3. Find examples of people who failed in their lives and later became successful. Try to find factors that account for these turnarounds.

Section | Six

CREATIVITY IN COUNSELING

A Fan of Garfield, Snoopy, Calvin and Hobbes
He names his erasers after one he called "Bob"
And further stimulates our sensations
By using his growing imagination

—Gladding, © 2000[5]

Counseling is both an art and a science. It is art in regard to timing and innovative as well as pragmatic actions. It is science in regard to research that supports the effectiveness of theories and techniques. Counselors are not effective if they lean too heavily in one direction or another. If they think of themselves as mainly artists, they have no substantive support for what they do. If they are just scientists, they may become "wooden" in their actions and interactions. Therefore, a balance between art and science is called for.

In this section, creativity is explored in and outside of counseling relationships. Counselors need to entertain creativity or they risk burning out, drying up, or being ineffective.

chapter 47

Socks

I once had the challenge of working with a woman who swore she would not change. She had been to the best and the brightest of counselors, she stated, and none of them had been helpful. She was fixated on being unhappy. Quite frankly, I thought she was coming to me in order to put another mark on her memory of misery the way gunfighters used to notch their guns. However, I was determined, so we started a counseling relationship. As she predicted, I had zero success with her. For every move and suggestion I made, she had a countermove. I probed. I confronted. I reinforced. I reflected. I empathized. Nothing happened. Finally, after several sessions and no progress, I realized the inevitable. She had "won."

Rather than be passive or aggressive about the matter, I became aware that I needed to do something to commemorate the event. Thus, as we were about to end another frustrating session, I reached down, untied my shoes, took off my socks, and handing them to her, I said, "You have won, and as a symbol of your victory, you shall have my socks. They are the modern equivalent of a sword or a shield that was given in antiquity to the victor at the end of a struggle. I want you to take them and display them on the mantel over your fireplace like a trophy. Then you can tell others of your hard work and what it led to. But please," I said, "just don't mention my name. I have a reputation in the community, and I don't like to admit failure."

She was stunned. She did not want to take the socks, but I was aware that somehow she must. So I persisted and insisted. She laughed. Then she did a strange and wonderful thing: She cried. She cried, and she cried, and she cried. When the tears stopped flowing, the words began to tumble out. She became more in tune with the feelings inside of her and acted on them. We extended that session, and we scheduled more. She got better.

She still has my socks as far as I know. They are somewhere in a frame in her house as a symbol of her transformation.

chapter 48

The Foxhole

Basic training in the Army is unique! It is filled with early morning exercise, long marches, night maneuvers, bivouacs, jumping off towers, cleaning brass, PT (physical training), KP (kitchen patrol), and learning how to fire a rifle. It is this latter experience that sticks out in my mind from the weeks I spent going through this once-in-a-lifetime-thank-God experience.

If you are not familiar with how the Army conducts its training, I can fill you in. It is by-the-numbers! Everything is coolly calculated and carried out in a precision manner. So it was with learning how to fire a rifle. Our platoon was marched out to the firing range and lined up. The group was then instructed on the nomenclature of the weapon we were to fire. We were told the difference between a rifle and a gun (a subject I would rather not dwell on). We were then shown how to fire our rifles at a target by an instructor who positioned himself in a foxhole.

After all of the finer points connected with firing a rifle had been made and reinforced at least thrice, we were ordered to line up before pre-dug foxholes, given ammunition clips, and told to take our rifles and set up in a firing position within the foxholes before us. All went well until I was ready to set up. At that point the bottom fell out for me, literally and figuratively. For when I jumped into my foxhole, I quickly realized I could not see over the top.

"A mighty big fox must have dug this hole," I mused.

But I did not have long to ponder the situation. For I heard the voice of the firing instructor yell, "Ready on the right?" which meant was everyone in position on the right side of him. Thus being on the left and not wanting to be left out or disgraced, I dug my boots into the side of the hole and shimmed up just in time to hear, "Ready on the left?" with an affirmative response.

All would have gone well had it not been for the next command, "Commence firing!"

Not placing the butt of the rifle up against my shoulder as instructed, I experienced a kick, a flick backwards, and a soft thud as I illustrated several laws of physics simultaneously. I could only pray no one saw me disappear from sight. Quickly, I scrambled up the sides again only to go through the same scenario a couple of more times when I forgot the correct procedure for firing my rifle.

The other most outstanding memory of my foxhole experience was climbing out after firing and going over my score with the instructor assigned to me. I did not hit the target that often. Then, as now, I can only imagine that my shots were such that had the possible adversary been riding Shetland ponies, I might have been a hero. However, such was not the case and my first foxhole adventure provided me with an opportunity to receive extra practice later until at last I actually earned a "marksman" rating.

While we in counseling do not follow the numbers in our work like the Army, we do count on theories and processes to guide us. Yet, we must be creative as well. We must make allowances for people who do not fit well into the client mode or who do not function adequately in society or therapy. That is hard to do. It is much easier to label those who come seeking help from us as "non-standard," "resistant," or "defiant." Yet, most can learn not just to compensate but to find satisfaction with themselves, others, and with life. Because of its nature, military commands have to operate in what some would call rigid and uniform ways but we, as counselors, do not have to. By seeing the uniqueness of everyone, we are free to attend to their needs. By so doing we can bring out the best in them. There are no foxholes in counseling.

chapter 49

Pantomime Can Be Powerful

While teaching a counseling course in Vienna, Austria, I decided to meet a friend in Prague for the weekend. He was more of an expert on Europe than I was and he suggested a timetable and a train. It seemed simple and straightforward.

First, I had to find from which station my train departed. Vienna has four. I investigated and found it would leave from the south terminal. Then I had to map and time my way from the house I was living in to the station. I actually did that a couple of ways and by the morning of my departure, I felt quite confident, maybe even a little cocky.

Therefore, I was surprised when I bought my ticket to find that I had to change trains after I crossed the Austrian border. "How bad can that be?" I thought, so nonchalantly I bought my ticket with great expectations. All went well initially. My train compartment traveler was a Latin teacher at a university in the Czech Republic. She got off at the same station I did and since everything was written in Czech (an alphabet quite different from the one I am used to), she told me from which platform my train would leave. To double check, I asked a policeman as well. He confirmed the scholar's instruction, so I happily hopped on board the train parked at Platform 4. It was a mistake!

The train I was supposed to take was at Platform 6 and left about 15 minutes before the train I was on. Therefore, when I handed my ticket to the conductor she looked at me with surprise and shook her head from side to side. She only spoke Czech and no one around spoke English. I only spoke English. However, I knew a little German. "Prague" (which is an English spelling of the word), I said, and followed it with the question "Nein?" as I hunched my shoulder.

"Nein!" she said straightforwardly and with authority.

"Oh...." I groaned, grimaced, and put my hand on my head shaking it from side to side.

I think she then asked me in Czech how the heck I got on a local train to Ceska Trebova instead of the one that went to Praha (i.e., Prague). All I could say was "Huh" (which meant simultaneously "I don't know," "The Latin teacher told me so," and "We have had a real break-down in communications here").

She seemed to get the message and gave me a hand signal that she would be back in a minute. Sure enough in just a flash she returned with another conductor, who after speaking to me in Czech, realized the American before her was completely lost and maybe lacking in a number of ways, including language skills and geographic intelligence. However, she and her companion knew enough German that combined with my German meant the three of us could work out a new schedule. (Actually, I mostly watched.)

At the next station, which was a rural stop, the conductors "escorted me" off the train, gave me the paper with the German words for cities in the Czech Republic, and with grim looks on their faces waved goodbye. I smiled, waved goodbye, and thought that I might never see Prague, Vienna, North Carolina, or my family again. I was literally on a weathered wooden platform in the middle of nowhere with a few chickens, amber waves of wheat fields all around, and a small station with an attendant who did not understand German or English or my former conductor friends. I literally surmised that the movie town in Bolivia where Butch Cassidy and the Sundance Kid had landed after leaving the Wild West had been transported somehow to the Czech Republic.

However, I showed the station manager the paper I had, pointed to myself, then pointed to the word *Praha*, and pointed in the direction I thought Praha was. He was most kind and pointed me to the door, used his fingers to count to 30, pointed to his watch, and took me to a place to stand. I did so at attention, as in the military. Then he waved goodbye (as if he were the resurrected captain of the Titanic), and I saluted.

Thirty minutes later, a train came and I marched on board stiff as a board and woodenly handed my ticket to the conductor. He smiled, and with an open hand gestured for me to take a seat. The rest of the trip was easy until I found out that Prague had two train stations. My hunch that the bigger station was the one I wanted to get off on paid off. I met my friend and we toured the city.

Later, frazzled, a bit bedazzled, and certainly grateful for getting to Prague, I swore I would never travel again without picking up more language skills ... and a cell phone! Pantomime can be powerful but it will only get you so far in life!

chapter 50

The Phony Prisoner

I've lived in six different states during my lifetime. Moving, like aging, is not always a smooth or easy process. Saying "goodbyes" and "hellos" can be awkward as well as painful.

In the midst of the noise and activity that accompany such transitions, there is silence. The silence, if extended, can be disturbing and discouraging. I found this fact out when I moved from North Carolina to Connecticut. My new environment was full of potential and difficulties I never imagined. My residence was in a neighborhood where people valued their privacy. Thus, meeting my neighbors, let alone greeting or interacting with them regularly, was a nonevent; that is, it did not happen. My colleagues at work were professionally friendly, but none of them lived near me, and our relationships ended when the workday did. The small town where I lived did not have singles groups or other activity groups that I could gravitate toward. Thus, as time went on, I realized I was isolated. What a strange feeling. I was used to being social and actively involved in various projects.

"What do I do now?" was the reoccurring thought that crossed my mind. My situation is not going to change soon. As I thought, I continued to read. It was the time right after the Iranian hostage crisis of the 1980s. Then one day, as I put down the newspaper, I picked up my pen.

"Although I am not in the same dire straits as those Americans who were held hostage," I thought, "I am in a crisis that I do not have great control over. I can respond positively to life as Victor Frankl advocated, or I can get depressed. The former sounds better." Thereafter, for almost a year, I pretended I was a prisoner in my house and that I had control over only paper, a pen, and any ideas I could generate.

I ritualistically wrote each day as I reflected on what I had read in counseling and what was occurring in my own life. The results were several manuscripts that were later published, as well as a habit I came to value. In 1999, I was cited as being in the top 1% of contributors to the *Journal of Counseling & Development* for the 15-year period from 1978 to 1993. Such a citation probably would not have happened had I not been in such dire straits and responded as I did. What we choose to do at any one time affects much of who we become and what our choices are later.

chapter | 51

The Words Are There/I Don't Know Where

She grew up in a family in which there was rampant alcohol abuse and neglect. So although she was polite and attractive, her self-concept was quite low. When she came to me, at the age of 23, she had already been through two marriages and numerous bad relationships. Therefore, she was hesitant to talk. After all, I was another man in her life, a life in which men had been and basically still were diabolical.

Yet, even in the first session I sensed that she knew I was genuinely interested in helping her. There was a glimmer of trust in her eyes. So at the end of the session I said, "Do you write?"

Her eyes brightened and widened. "Yes," she quietly replied.

"Well, how about writing some of your thoughts this week. You could read them to me next time and that way you would not have to depend on me for questions. You would be in charge." She agreed.

The next week she came in with a couplet that she read to start the session.

The words are there
I don't know where.

To my surprise and I think hers too, she then began to talk about how hard it was to talk. She was especially reluctant to discuss herself, she said, because she really was not important. Yet, she talked about herself, and as her words came out the conversation deepened. Thus, from the initial couplet came thoughts, feelings, and experiences.

She continued to write and became even more spontaneous and open in her speech, especially about herself. Her candor produced clarity, and for the first time in her life she was able to see herself as something other than a victim.

At our last session, she brought in a final couplet. It read as follows:

As I now enjoy and experience the earth
I feel as if I've gone through a total rebirth.
Indeed, she had. Writing led to relaxation, which led to insight,

which led to openness and growth. The power of the words helped her raise herself out of despair and depression. Jotting down thoughts is like jogging down trails. Both are therapeutic for those seeking to live healthy lives.

chapter 52

Nothing Could be Finer ... Almost!

$\mathcal{W}$ hen I made my plane reservations to go as an external evaluator for a counseling program in Malaysia, I did so with cost in mind. I wanted to get the least expensive round trip ticket that got me from Winston-Salem, North Carolina, to Kuala Lumpur in the shortest time. Therefore, I chose a cheap air website and purchased tickets. For a low price I was to go from Dulles Airport in northern Virginia through Beijing to my final destination. I was not sure exactly what to expect, but I thought that since I was "passing through" China I would have little trouble going through the airport. I could not have been more wrong!

The first clue I had that the situation might be more challenging than I expected was when I asked my flight attendant if there would be good signage at the airport. She was "not sure" and asked the senior member of the crew who was "not sure" either. "No problem," I thought. "I have transferred through airports dozens of times and never had difficulty."

That was the last positive thought I had for awhile. Signage was available when I entered the airport and it was in English as well as Chinese. However, my airline was not listed as one to which I could transfer. So I went up to the "Information for Transfer to Foreign Airports" booth and asked the attendant what to do. Her words were simple. She instructed me to go straight and stand in the last line in the airport lobby. I did as she told me but noticed the sign above the line was blurred. Furthermore, my fellow liners were all bound for stays in China. Something must be wrong, I surmised. Complicating the matter even more, the line was moving at a snail's pace. There were 50 people in front of me and it was taking about 5 minutes for each person to get through. I had only 90 minutes to make my connection. Quickly calculating the situation in front of me, I knew it would take me over 2 hours to move through. By then my flight would have taken off. I needed to do something and quickly if I was not to be left behind.

Then I noticed a big sign to my left. It said "Transfers to Foreign Airports" and underneath it were the letters "D/P" (which I later found out stood for "Diplomatic Passport"). I was inspired and moved into the D/P line faster than anyone might say "Henry Kissinger." There were only about a dozen people ahead of me, so I patiently waited my turn as the length of the line shortened ever so slowly. When at last I was called up to meet and greet the inspector, I had less than a half an hour before my flight would depart. Stoically, but with a smile, I presented my passport to a rather stern-looking young man in a military uniform. He looked at the passport, stared at me, and then examined the passport again.

With his head shaking from side to side he barked out in a very firm voice, "You're no diplomat!"

"He's right," I said to myself, "but I've really got to catch my flight or sleep in the airport tonight," so I calmly replied, "But I'm diplomatic and I always use this line every time I come through the Beijing airport." (Both were true.)

The inspector looked at me harshly, unsympathetically, skeptically, gruffly, roughly, and then with a light flip of his wrist and a hint of a smile stamped my passport.

I said, "Thank you very much" about a dozen times, at the end of which I began to sound like Elvis Presley.

With 10 minutes left, I raced in the direction that everyone else was going until I found a uniformed information agent, slipped him a $20 bill, and said in a low and sincere tone, "Help me," which was exactly what he did. To this day, I will never really know how the agent made time stand still, persuaded the airline officials at Malaysian Airlines to open back up, and got the bureaucratic baggage inspectors to let my earthly belongings travel with me. But it happened and I arrived in Kuala Lumpur on time.

In retrospect, I realize I was fortunate. However, I also am aware I did some things to help myself. I got out of a line that was going nowhere fast and into one that had promise. I was patient, proactive, humorous in regard to my plight, creative in my responses to circumstances, asked for help, and provided resources for my final helper who got me off the ground. Had I gotten upset, lashed out in anger, been impatient, called people names, or acted passively, I might still be in Beijing today.

In counseling, the same is true about moving from a current situation into the future. Sometimes our clients are desperate and in despair. They rail and wail against life circumstances when they have the ability to be constructive and move on. In such situations, the ways we help them are connected to those we use to help ourselves when we are surrounded by chaos and systems we do not understand.

Instead of just accepting the inevitable of whatever may come, we need to help those with whom we work read the signs, make the moves, and see what can be beyond the present. That calls for probing, persistence, and reinforcement of clients who take risks. As the lyrics about the states of Carolina say, "nothing could be finer," to which I would add, "unless it's using your wit to change planes in China!"

Points to Ponder

1. When have you been creative in your thoughts or actions? How did such times make a difference in your life?

2. What could you do to be more playful or divergent in your life? Be as specific as you can (e.g., traveling to another country, reading an inspiring book, playing games with adults or children).

3. Look for stories on-line, in newspapers, or in magazines that highlight the creativity of individuals or groups. Think of what they did and how they did it and try to imagine how what you read might apply to certain counseling situations.

MULTICULTURAL AND SPIRITUAL CONSIDERATIONS

With age she has learned
to forgive the groups
that mistreated her
because of her color.
Each Saturday she now bakes bread
and takes it to the local mission
where she stays to cut and serve it
with love and a main dish.
Her grace has overcome years of hatred,
angry words, and hours of sadness.
Her brightness exudes a subtle warmth.
Everyone calls her "Rainbow."

—Gladding, 1999[6]

The earth is not only constantly in motion but also changing. The heroes of yesterday are not the same as today. The mixture of the population differs, too. In the United States, for instance, people of color are quietly becoming a majority. This type of change gives us pause because we sometimes hang on to the past in the hope that it will become the future. Yet, the only secure knowledge we have is that change is inevitable and sometimes it accelerates to become something we never expected. That is why being sensitive to other cultures outside of one's own is crucial to being an effective counselor.

The stories in this section emphasize the appreciation of life beyond limited cultural boundaries. What we do in regard to this phenomenon has implications for both how we counsel and how we live. Ask yourself as you read, what experiences have you had outside of your level of cultural comfort, and how have they affected you?

An Encounter With the Klan

I can still remember hearing the car horns in the distance. They were coming. The Ku Klux Klan was holding a rally on the courthouse square of my hometown of Decatur, Georgia, and they were driving up Church Street in front of my house as a part of their route. I was 10 years old, and up to that point my family had tried to protect me as much as possible from the sounds and the sights of the divided society that was the South of the 1950s. That summer day was no exception as my father quickly shooed me inside. Innocence was about to be lost, and he knew it. Yet, he tried as best he could to keep my brother, my sister, and me as far removed as possible from the evil that was to pass before us.

In retrospect, I am sure he thought of sending us away for the day. However, he probably knew that such a tactic would backfire later. There was no escape from the pervasiveness of racism that dominated southern culture at the time. It was simply accepted and legally codified. Blacks and Whites were different races that should be kept separate and segregated from each other because Blacks were perceived as inferior. That view covered everything in its day like kudzu and strangled out reasonable discussions and change. So, as the car horns became louder and the Klan caravan drew closer, I was confined to the screened-in front porch of our house to watch silently a noisy parade full of people in hoods, Confederate battle flags, and the screaming of words that were offensive. The instructions from my father were clear: "You may look," he told me, "but you must remain as still as the humid air."

My wait was not long in coming, but while I sat, I thought as well as anticipated. I had read about the Klan and its origin. I knew that Nathan Bedford Forrest had founded the Klan in Tennessee after the Civil War to suppress the freedom of Blacks and keep them fearful and subservient to Whites. I had read of a recent Klan rally and cross burning at nearby Stone Mountain on a Saturday night in the Sunday edition of *The Atlanta Journal-Constitution* that I helped my brother deliver. I was not as naive as my father thought or wished. Yet, I did not know anyone who was an affiliate or advocate for the Klan or its causes. That made sense because the group was one surrounded by secrecy. You became a target of its wrath only if you spoke out against what it tried to enforce by intimidation and murder. So, I sat quietly and watched as the first cars came by. I was to see what I had read about up close and face-to-face.

However, what happened was different from what I had envisioned. The distance from our porch to the street was about 50 feet, so I had a clear view. What surprised me was what I saw. Before me were people in vehicles who were faceless in the sense that I could not see who they were. It was like Halloween in the summertime. Over their heads were white sheets shaped in the form of hoods that prevented anyone from identifying them. Instead, from the holes in their masks I caught glimpses of faces—eyes, noses, and mouths—but nothing distinctive. Even more striking was the fact that as these people passed our house, they not only blew their horns but also waved. I was confused. I thought evil should look and act like evil. Here before me was the personification of prejudice waving enthusiastically and in a friendly manner. Something was disturbingly wrong with the picture.

However, I did as instructed. I did not move a muscle for fear that my father would punish me. The whole parade lasted only about five minutes. Then the honking of car horns and the white-robed, faceless people disappeared from my immediate senses as they became lodged in my memory.

In reflecting on this one moment in time, I realize that that day and my internal reaction to the events before me have continued to have an impact on my life both personally and professionally. For one thing, I saw then, and see even more clearly now, that racism is often faceless and parades around as if it were something else. The camouflage of racism and its pretentious nature makes it elusive and difficult to get a handle on—let alone address constructively.

chapter 54

Shirley

$\mathcal{S}$he was an older woman seated in the middle of my Monday night class on introduction to counseling. She stood out in both her manner and looks—well-dressed and gray-haired in the midst of blue jeans and youth. I glanced at her, smiled, and thought to myself, "She doesn't have a prayer."

It wasn't that I knew this woman. It was that I had known other older women. I had had them in my classes before in North Carolina and in Connecticut. I knew they had to be the same in Alabama. These women were usually not my best students. In fact, I could easily think of half a dozen examples of older women who had gotten my past classes off track by making comments related to anything but the materials we were studying. I could also think of many tests on which these women had not been clear, concise, or articulate about counseling.

Now please understand, I had a great love for my Grandmother Templeman, a woman whom we had called "Pal" as children and who was sharp mentally until her death at age 87. I also appreciated and admired the kindness of other older women I had encountered in church and in civic life. It seems they were always generous to a fault with mint candies in their purses and with nurturing words. These were strong women who combined goodness with kindness. Yet, give me an older woman in class, and I cringed because of my past experiences. The combination seemed to be like poetry and power tools. They just did not seem to go together.

But instead of fantasizing about how this older woman would do, I decided to face my bias and find out something about her as the rest of the class arrived. I introduced myself and then said, "Who are you?"

"My name is Shirley Ratliff," she replied, without volunteering any other information.

"Welcome to the class," I said, and then in a more direct way than is usually my manner (and that must have reflected prejudice), I queried, "Why are you here?"

"I want to learn how to be a counselor" was her straightforward answer. "I've been volunteering at sites that require counseling skills. I want to learn how to do things right and be a professional."

"If you work hard, you will learn," I assured her, wanting to believe my own words and transcend obvious doubts. Thus ended my first conversation with Shirley, a person to whom I would later dedicate a book because I admired her so much.

So why do I tell you this story? The answer I think is because Shirley was the antithesis of all my preconceived ideas. She was bright, witty, articulate, and thoughtful. To this day I consider her to be the epitome of what a counseling student should be. If it had not been for Shirley, my life experience would be much poorer. Worse yet, I would still harbor a bias against the potency of older women.

chapter 55

WASPs

I can still hear her opening words as we sat down in the corner office overlooking the parking lot.

"I don't like WASPs!" she said emphatically.

She was African American, and here I was as White Anglo-Saxon Protestant (WASP) as they came. In addition, I was male, which I am sure was not a factor in my favor.

"Didn't anybody screen this client?" I thought. "Why was she given to me? What am I going to do now?"

"I don't like WASPs," she repeated as forcefully as her first statement. (I did not need to be reminded, but she continued.) "They are awful! They get in your face. They get in your hair. I don't know why the Good Lord made them."

"I don't think I am being affirmed here," I said silently to myself. "There are some real feelings coming from this client, and I have yet to utter a word."

However, since the subject had come up, I asked her, "Tell me more about WASPs and your dislike for them."

She stared at me in disbelief, as if to say, "What am I not conveying about my disdain for WASPs?"

However, after a brief pause she said, looking up, "As a little girl I was stung a number of times by them. Our house, like your office, had lots of them in it."

Her words and her look caught my attention. She was not talking about a group of people. She was talking about insects, and as I looked at the windows, which she could see more clearly than me, I realized fully the reason she had begun our session as she had. There must have been at least half dozen wasps behind the blinds. It did not take 20/20 vision to see them outlined by the sun, flying in short bursts.

I immediately called downstairs to find a new room for counseling and to alert the secretary that we needed to call a pest control company. As we sat down in our new quarters I also confessed my thoughts to the woman in front of me. She was kind in her remarks, although she quickly revealed that she had suffered insults, discrimination, and indignation from White, Protestant men in her life and wondered why she had been matched up with me. I offered to find her someone new, but after addressing the issue, she wanted to go ahead with the session. We did, and her difficulty, which focused on a child, was a matter that was eventually resolved.

However, what sticks in my mind to this day is the fact that if the office I chose to work in had not had insects in the window, I might be less sensitive now to cultures and to how my own background heritage influences what I do in counseling sessions. WASPs and wasps can be beneficial. However, they can also be frightening and dangerous. Who we are and how we look affects others on multiple levels.

chapter 56

The Argentine

At one time in my life, I was a soccer coach for my middle son's nine-year-old team. The league we played in was not that competitive, but I was. Therefore, when a league official called to inform me that I had a late addition to my roster, I was delighted to hear that the boy was from Argentina.

"Just what the team needs!" I thought. "With Juan we will win and everyone will be happy!"

Therefore, at the next scheduled practice, I showed up early to welcome the new arrival. I met his mother first. She was gracious and appreciative of our including her son on the "Stars" roster.

"What position does he play?" I inquired.

"Any position you want him to try" was the response.

Then I looked at Juan. He was tall and wiry with chiseled features and a look of determination in his eye.

"Are you ready to kick a few?" I questioned.

"Yes," he said, "as soon as I take off my warm-ups and adjust my braces."

"Why do you need to adjust your braces?" I asked. "We don't chew gum during games and we certainly won't be chewing on any balls today."

He smiled and said, "I need to fix my leg braces."

Well, the words *leg braces* were not what I had expected from the mouth of this young man. Regardless of the hope I had carried with me up to this point in time, the reality of the situation appeared right before me when Juan removed his sweats and showed me the steel that supported his legs. With a hop, skip, and run gait he ran out to join the other boys and my dreams and fantasies fled from my mind, as the reality of talent that I saw was less than stellar.

Even though Juan did not lead our team on to victory, he did become a valued member of the group. He was spirited if not swift. He tried hard and held his ground. He played every minute of every game to the best of his ability.

Multicultural and Spiritual Considerations

From the experience, I learned anew not to stereotype or to expect too much from hearsay or fantasy. While many children in Argentina love soccer and play it well, there are many who do not or cannot. That is to be expected. It is only when we try to make people something they are not that we had better brace ourselves for disappointment. At any age, people will be who they can be and no wish can make them more!

chapter 57

Spirits, Spirituality, and Counseling

I had only one item with me that day in the grocery store line. It was a bottle of wine. I was going to a newly married couple's home, and I wanted to take them a present. I was pleased that I had remembered to stop and get them a gift. What I did not notice was that I had forgotten to take off my nametag from work. I was doing a clinical internship in the chaplain's department at a local hospital. It was an exciting opportunity, and I was learning a lot about counseling and spirituality. However, when I presented the bottle of wine to the cashier, she looked at me disapprovingly after reading my nametag. When I realized what was happening, I tried to make light of the whole situation.

"Would you believe this wine is for communion?" I inquired.

"When did white wine start making it to the altar?" she countered.

"How about medical purposes?"

"What ails you?" she retorted. "We have a complete pharmacy department in this store."

"Actually, this wine is for a newly married couple," I confessed.

"They don't need it," was all she could say. "Save it for when they get old and are not so peppy."

Well, I bought the wine, received my change, and hurried out the door slightly embarrassed, wishing I had the bag she had put the bottle in over my head instead.

Spirituality and counseling is not a story about wine or presents. Rather, it is an emphasis within the profession on helping people become more aware of their spiritual side as a part of their lives. That process is easier for some to check out than for others, but it is a vital dimension of counseling, whether one works in a chaplain's department or in a more secular setting.

chapter 58

Becoming a Student of Culture

I n the hard work of becoming a counselor, we must be prepared to be a student (i.e., a learner), regardless of our age or status. It is when we have the openness and eagerness for new knowledge that we are best able to make the most of our experiences. For example, I remember when I went to Calcutta, India, to work with Mother Teresa in the mid-1990s, I thought I was prepared and would not be shocked or taken aback by what I saw. After all, I had seen poor people struggle daily while working in a rural mental health center in the 1970s. I had also taken several courses dealing with death and dying and had led grief groups.

However, Calcutta was different. People were living on the streets with nothing over their heads except plastic tarps if they were lucky. On almost every corner were truly needy and hungry individuals. There were also people literally dying in those same streets daily. The following thoughts sum up my first impressions:

Our band of seekers
wanders out into the streets of Calcutta
hesitantly, with a touch of anxiety.
As a veteran traveler I am calm
sure within myself
that I will be safe from the shock of anything that might be new.
At every corner and in between are
beggars, butchers,
and sellers of "things."
At every turn and in straight-aways
harsh realities come alive.
There is a dead dog next to a girl drawing pictures
a deformed old man talking nonsense to himself
the foul smells and loud sounds of taxis and rickshaws

a horde of flies and human feces on mounds of trash.
Amid the crowd, odors of food,
and looks of desperation emerge.
I am not shocked — just stunned (in denial)
My senses have been overwhelmed.

The first time I stepped over a dead body I knew my previous knowledge had not translated or transferred well. I had to learn anew in order to be genuinely helpful. It was a humbling but most meaningful experience.

Since that time I have thought that becoming a counselor or a person in new surroundings may involve as much setting aside past learning as incorporating present realities. Even when we are in similar environments, we must be open to facts and people we do not know. Then and only then can we ever hope to be able to do much good.

chapter 59

Putting on the Gloves With Mother Teresa

In December 1995 I took a group of Wake Forest undergraduates to Calcutta, India, to work in the homes of Mother Teresa. It was a moving and uplifting experience, spiritual in the best sense of that word as our small band mixed daily with Muslims, Hindus, Christians, and others who lived and worked in the places where we volunteered. Along the way I had the privilege of actually meeting Mother Teresa, who both looked like her pictures (small, frail, stooped, and wrinkled) and lived up to her reputation. She literally broke off conversation with our group to go clean toilets.

However, what I remember most about my three weeks in the City of Joy was the work I did in the homes, especially the daily bathing of sick and infirmed men at Prem Dan, a home for those who are too physically and mentally disabled to take care of themselves. The men were just getting ready for their baths when I arrived each morning. Many were in wheelchairs, some were on crutches, and a number were mobile but a bit shaky on their feet.

The only hot water for bathing was boiled over a stove in large kettles. There was never enough of it, and cold water rinses and full, cold baths were mostly the norm. The most labor-intensive part of the bathing process, though, was getting the night clothes off of the men and scrubbing down those too infirm to do so for themselves. On numerous occasions, I not only removed clothing but also scraped dried feces from these men's buttocks and legs. That job was never pleasant but was always necessary. To be safe, I wore latex gloves and would say to myself as the work began, "I'm putting on the gloves with Mother Teresa" (who I knew from my previous experience used gloves at times, too).

Other interactions with the men included shaving their heads as a preventive way of dealing with lice and shaving their faces so they would feel cleaner and more refreshed. Both jobs were done with razors that were anything but new and sharp. It was a grueling task and yet one I loved because the men seemed so appreciative even when I cut them (which unfortunately was often).

As I reflected then and now about my time in Calcutta, I think of how different and similar the work there was to the counseling I have done. The behavior of care was expressed physically and mostly nonverbally in India, whereas in the United States I have been mostly cognitive and verbal in what I have given to others. I could see my results immediately at Prem Dan, whereas in counseling I seldom see such tangible evidence. Yet in both cases, I knew that what I did made a difference. I also realized anew that helping is not one-dimensional.

I was blessed to enter the lives of some downtrodden men in the middle of the last decade of the 20th century. They taught me gratitude for the circumstances of my own life, but more importantly, helped me see and feel life more fully. Calcutta embodied the worst of human life, yet paradoxically it brought out the best within me and others who shared the experience. What a surprise!

chapter 60

Getting There

*K*nowledge is important in our society because it helps inform and direct. Without knowledge, we misunderstand and are mis- understood. This fact became personalized in my life one June day in Calais, France. It was before the opening of the English/French tunnel, and I was waiting with a friend to catch a boat back to Dover. It was hot, and to pass the time we read whatever we could find. All of a sudden, my friend became excited as he pointed to a sign.

"Look," he said. "We are going to have problems. We are taking a boat to Britain with people who are mentally and physically limited."

I glanced up to read the words announcing this phenomenon for my- self. Sure enough, on the schedule chart was the name of our boat, and out by the side of it was the word *retarded*, that is, delayed. Knowing just a bit of French I was able to tell my friend that he should be more wor- ried about his inability to understand a foreign language than the type of passengers onboard our ship.

Getting somewhere in counseling is based on knowledge. However, sometimes because of unforeseen events we may be delayed in acquiring information as rapidly as would be ideal. At such times, we may become frustrated because of the delay. If we know that fact before departing into the uncharted waters of change and clients, we will be calmer and the process will go more smoothly, even if it is slower.

chapter 61

Ten Pesos for the Gringo

I have attended the International Association for Counselling (IAC) Conferences several times. I have found them all informative and worthwhile. I have learned much. However, one of the most valuable lessons I have learned from these meetings is to come prepared. That knowledge came as a result of my first experience in traveling to the conference. It was in Buenos Aires.

When I arrived, I realized I needed to exchange money but I did not do so because the fellow counselors I was with were going straight to our hotel and there simply was not time. Having settled in, I decided to go to meetings that were a taxi ride away. When I got in the taxi, I had yet to go to the bank. However, thinking that my driver might even prefer United States currency, I just gave him the address of the venue and sat back.

When we arrived, he stated that the fare was 10 pesos. I knew the exchange rate and offered him more in United States money. He looked surprised, then a little angry, and then he was very insistent that I pay him in pesos. Nothing I could do or say would change his mind and as we talked the doors were locked. "Uh, oh," I thought. "This is not a good sign."

I also thought I might ask him if he would wait for me to go around the corner to a bank. However, that thought quickly left my mind as I realized anything resembling trust was not with in the confines of the car.

Then, seemingly out of nowhere, but actually from a nearby building stepped Courtland Lee, the future president of IAC. Courtland was a friend, and testing friendship to its limit, I yelled, "Courtland, do you have 10 pesos for a gringo (the term that my lack of sensitivity had made me)?"

Thank heaven, he did. I think he even gave the driver a little tip and I would not have been surprised had he offered me one. However, I knew he knew I had learned a valuable lesson.

Pesos, euros, pounds, dollars, and those change denominations that go with them not only have a value in specific countries but they are a source of pride for many people. Like speaking another's language, those who differ from us want us to respect their way of life. One way to do that is to be current in their currency. Another way is to observe traditions and respect rituals and ways of working in the world. To not think ahead is to dread what happens later. Locked doors or closed minds do nothing to promote the well-being of anyone. When traveling or counseling, it is vital to do so from a common-ground approach. This often means that we as counselors must make the first move. To do less is to court disaster and there are only so many Courtland Lees that can and do come to our rescue.

chapter | 62

Geography and Identity

$\mathcal{W}$e do not get a choice as to where we are born anymore than we get to select our parents. Yet our ideas and identity are shaped by both.

I was born in Atlanta, 80 years after the Civil War ended. My parents were transplanted Virginians who arrived in the city from Richmond because my father was transferred there by his company during the 1940s. Every day of my developing years was a history lesson, not only because of my ancestry, but because of the love my parents and grandmother had of telling stories about "The War" and its aftereffects. Plus, there were still veterans from that conflict alive and kicking. Geographically, too, Georgia had been a battlefield state and the Battle of Atlanta had been one of its most decisive and significant clashes with the results propelling Abraham Lincoln on to a second term in 1864.

So, I grew up Southern with all of its assets and liabilities. My hero, Robert E. Lee, was a distant relative. My mantra was "be polite, be well mannered, and be competitive." I loved the red, white, and blue—not of the United States flag—but of the stars and bars. I cringe now even writing these words but, in truth, that was who I was. My family was anything but affluent yet they were educated, mostly open-minded, and had high standards. I was loved even when I failed, but I realized early that it was important not to fail. When I did, I knew it was expected that I would be back in the fray again soon in order to succeed.

However, as I grew and the world of television news entered our living room, I became aware that despite the pride I carried in my heritage, Southerners were looked down on by the rest of the nation. Two reasons were apparent. First, Southerners were seen as backward. The sophisticated ones were believed to have moved out of the region. Second, segregation was seen, and rightfully so, as a scourge. Jim Crow laws separated people by outward appearance. More importantly, they treated a whole class of people inhumanely.

There was really not much I could do, when at age 15, the Civil Rights Movement exploded in the heart of Dixie. I followed the news with ambivalent feelings. I was still first and foremost a Southerner. However, through school and conversations outside of my house, I became more sensitized and began to change subtly at first and more dramatically later. The changes manifested themselves in my talk, but more importantly in my actions. I lived in an integrated neighborhood by choice as a college student. I attended Yale Divinity School, a hub of social action, when I could have easily gone to any other less dynamic divinity school. I returned to Connecticut to work after I completed my Ph.D. I even married a Nutmegger. My sensitivity to others outside my initial world later reached as far as Calcutta in working in the homes of Mother Teresa.

I relate all of this information to make a couple of points. First, unless exposed otherwise, people continue to be who their ancestors and geography dictate that they should be. Second, people can and do change when opportunities present themselves. The process is largely developmental as a comfort zone is left behind and new ideas are presented. The outcome can be transformative.

I value and embrace some of the lessons I gleaned from my childhood. Yet, as an adult, I am glad I have moved beyond the bands and bonds that held me in to a worldview that was constricting and confining. When we see clients, we need to remember who we were at one time as well as who they are. We also should be cognizant of how we have changed and what that experience was like. We need to realize that all regions of the country, and indeed the world, have a provincial nature about them. Our travels, real and imagined, can help us grow personally and culturally.

Our clients, like us, are in the process of change. Because they may not be enlightened or insightful today does not mean there is no hope for them tomorrow. Heredity and geography are formidable barriers to overcome and in most circumstances, the process of changing our worldview is slow, uneven, and difficult. Yet, when there are breakthroughs, they are exhilarating and worth waiting for. Not giving up or becoming cynical is key in allowing people to change.

chapter 63

Women Are People!

For a moment I could not believe my eyes. It was a bitter cold snowy winter's day in Ottawa, Canada, and I was looking at a group of bronze statues. There before me on Parliament Hill were the more-than-life-size figures of the Famous Five Canadian leaders: Emily Murphy, Nellie McClung, Irene Parlby, Louise McKinney, and Henrietta Muir Edwards. They led the struggle that ended on October 18, 1929, when women were legally declared persons under the British North America Act and made eligible for appointment to the Canadian Senate. In the hands of Nellie McClung is a newspaper with this headline: "Women are People," which reflects some of the actual headlines of Canadian papers of that day.

So why did that statue "grab me" emotionally whereas the other 16 outside of Parliament did not? I think because of the human rights and social justice nature of the monumental event it celebrated. I am always shocked when I see discrimination and oppression imposed on individuals because of factors that are either insignificant or over which they have no control. None of us voted before coming into this world whether we would be male or female, White or a person of color, tall or short, affluent or poor, able or disabled—the list goes on longer than the story of human existence. The point is that all of us are persons. It should not take a court decision to confirm or affirm that fact. When we pretend otherwise or set up systems to keep people down, we are not just hurting the people being held back. We are inflicting wounds on ourselves and society as well.

Women are people! African Americans are people! Lesbians and gay men are in this category, too, as are White guys, older adults, children, the creative, the mundane, the smart, the less talented, and the lame. Those on Wall Street and those who sweep the streets are a part of the chain that unite us as human beings. Our humanity crosses lines, and when we are in harmony with it, we become more "divine" in the best and fullest sense of that word.

In counseling, our clients are people. We should never forget that. They may hurt, abuse, be insightful, be capricious, or be clueless. Regardless of what they have, what they lack, what they bring, what they discover, or where they go, they share with us universal hopes, wishes, and ambitions for a good life and the freedoms that come with it. The Famous Five of Canada fought for a landmark decision. We who are less famous, but hopefully no less determined, should be decisive in advocating for the rights of all in and outside our professional domain. As Martin Luther King Jr. reminded us, "The time is always right to do the right thing."

Points to Ponder

1. What experiences do you have with people outside your immediate cultural group(s)? What opinions do you have of these people? Why?

2. Age discrimination is illegal but still occurs. Project your life 10 years from now. How would you like to be seen and treated?

3. Prejudice is usually subtle. Where have you seen prejudice in your environment, and how have you seen it effectively dealt with?

THE INFLUENCES OF COLLEAGUES, FRIENDS, AND FAMILY

I walk thoughtfully down Beecher Road
at the end of a summer of too little growth,
the autumn wind stirring around me,
orange remnants of once green leaves.
I am the son of a fourth-grade teacher
and a man who dabbled in business and roses,
a descendant of Virginia farmers
and open-minded Baptists,
the husband of a Connecticut woman,
the father of growing children.
Youngest of three, I am a trinity
counselor
teacher
writer.
Amid the cold, I approach home,
midlife is full of surprises.

—Gladding, 1998[7]

The influence of family, friends, and colleagues cannot be overestimated. These are the people whom we are closest to and most dependent on in life. They are the ones who are there for us when we are under stress and who rejoice with us when there are events to celebrate. These individuals listen to us, empathize with us, and know us best. If they are healthy and wise, we become better because of the association. If they are too absorbed in their own affairs, we and our relationships with them may suffer.

The Influences of Colleagues, Friends, and Family

The stories in this section are focused on events connected collectively with this group of people. As you read these vignettes try to remember times in your life when your family, friends, and colleagues have made a positive impact on what you did, thought, felt, or how you perceived a situation. What did they do? What did you learn and take away from the experience(s)?

chapter 64

The Office

*T*he first office I had as a clinician was in a room with two other people, a rehabilitation counselor and a substance abuse counselor. Each of us had a desk, a chair, and a lamp. The first one to arrive each morning turned on the overhead light, and the last one to leave at night flicked it off. When we had clients, the other two colleagues left. I learned to be adaptable quite early in my career and to conduct counseling sessions while sitting on stairs in a hallway or walking around a parking lot. However, I enjoyed working in the office. I always felt fortunate when my roommates either left it to me or were somewhere else. The office made me feel more professional.

Yet, I found out from this experience that offices are not as valuable as colleagues. There were numerous times when I consulted with each of them for information or strategies to use with my clients. They were gracious to a fault although they had their own peculiarities, such as the substance abuse counselor not being able to go for long periods of time without having a cup of coffee.

Since that early experience, I have been less impressed with my surroundings than with the people with whom I work. A desk, a chair, a lamp, and four walls are easy to replace. A sensitive and smart colleague is priceless, especially one who provides you with support and insight.

chapter 65

Happenstance: Note Whom You Quote

A presentation I made in 1979 was before the American Psychological Association's Division of Humanistic Psychology in New York City. At that time I had become intrigued, because of my clinical experiences, with the use of the arts in counseling, especially the use of poetry. Therefore, my presentation was on the use of poetry as therapy in counseling. I had abundant case examples, but I needed to have a better knowledge of the underlying theory on which my work was based. Fortunately for me, a book entitled *Poetry as Therapy* (Lerner, 1978) arrived about two months before my presentation. I had time to read it thoroughly and digest its contents before the convention. It was a jewel of a book. I remember how grateful I was for its timely publication.

Thus on a sunny September morning, I stood up to address about 25 people in a hotel suite at the Waldorf Astoria on a subject that I had an interest in and now had some background material on. As I began my remarks I told my audience how my clients often brought in or wrote poems during their counseling sessions and how I had found these poems to offer catharsis, insight, and relief. I then said that in addition to what I intuitively knew about the value of poetry, I had recently read a book on its uses in therapy.

"The author/editor of the book is a guy named Arthur Lerner from Los Angeles," I stated. "I don't know him. Does anybody?"

"I'm Lerner," piped up a balding older gentleman in the front row.

"You are?" I gulped. "Arthur Lerner, the author/editor of *Poetry as Therapy*?"

"The same," he responded.

"I hope I'm quoting you correctly," I replied.

"Go on," he gently commanded. And I did.

After the presentation, I received a number of immediate comments about what had been discussed, but none were from Arthur Lerner. Instead, he came up to me and asked, "What are you doing for dinner tonight?"

I was free, and so about 6 p.m. I found myself in his company, along with that of his wife, Matilda. We talked for several hours, and I received much food for thought as well as substance. The next week Art called me. We again discussed the use of poetry in the therapeutic process. Later he invited me out to California to do a workshop at UCLA, and a few years afterward I wrote a chapter for him in a book he edited on the uses of literature in the therapeutic experience. Until his death in 1997, Art was a close friend although we lived 3,000 miles apart. He introduced me to a larger world of counseling that I would never have been exposed to had he not befriended and mentored me.

I had no way of knowing that I would meet Arthur Lerner or that I would benefit so much from knowing him. I think that is the way it is with counseling sometimes too. People and words come to us, and in them and through them we are enriched as well as enrich others. There is no way of knowing when such times will come. It is all a delightful surprise of being a continuous learner.

chapter 66

Sources Within

One event in my life that created a crisis equal to those I have faced with many clients was a broken engagement. I was in my 20s at the time and had limited knowledge and skill. It was an event I wish had never happened because of the psychological pain I went through. Yet in retrospect, what I learned from the breakup probably changed the course of my life for the better. As with anyone who has gone through the dissolving of an intimate relationship, I was not immune to the turmoil of conflicting feelings that tossed about and numbed my mind as well as penetrated through the very fiber of my body and into my bones. Termination came, and reality sank in. Depression became a dull constant companion. I was not near family or friends. Rather, I was isolated. In my initial attempts to get past the situation, I found myself talking to those whom I knew around me. However, reaching out on my part did not produce anything positive.

"So what do I do now?" I thought. There was no clear answer or direction. No signal, sign, or inspiration came. I waited, feeling fatigued, discouraged, hopeless, and abandoned. In the midst of this time, one night I went to sleep and really wondered what I would do the next day if things were not better. That night I had a dream like none I have had before or since. In the dream I saw myself in a desert. I could feel the hot sand beneath me, see the bleak landscape before me, and even feel a dryness in my throat. I actually felt myself crawling along. I remember wondering, "Will I live through this experience?"

At a point where I put my head down in the sand and was about to give up, a strange thing happened. Out of nowhere, four of my ancestors appeared on the scene. I did not know but one of them personally, my Grandmother Templeman who had died a few years before. However, I recognized all of the people from my family's historical past by name and face, for I had seen their pictures in frames in our house and heard stories about them that had been told to me as a child. I did not move, but I remember my grandmother saying, "You're exhausted. We'll carry you until you're able to walk again." And with that, they lifted me up.

From that moment on I knew I would make it through the trauma I was facing and that my life would eventually be okay. I also knew I would get through the pain of the crisis I was in and that regardless of what events happened in the future, I would get through them as well. I have. It is not that life has been easy. It has not. But I know that from struggle and pain, inner resources can come into play and outer resources can be tapped so that in the midst of angst, anxiety, or despondency, we can become different in a better—not a bitter—way.

chapter 67

Cool Under Fire

*M*y work as a counselor has sometimes taken me on the road. In such cases, I have often timed my out-of-the-office experiences to coincide with an opportunity to have lunch with someone. On one such occasion I met a rehabilitation counselor who was a good friend.

As we sat eating our blue-plate specials of barbecue in a greasy restaurant, we discussed different aspects of being a counselor. The conversation included a wide range of topics from diagnosis to burnout. We were intensely involved in our discussion in the back of the seating area away from others and were engrossed in our own little world. Thus, we were annoyed at the close, loud sound of sirens from the outside. However, they stopped, and we continued with our dialogue, which was at times a bit hot and heavy.

Finally, I got up to get some water because no waitress had come by in a while. As I left our area I found more than I was looking for. Several firemen were entering the building with hoses. (I knew they could spare some water, but I did not ask.)

During our conversation a small kitchen fire had started. We had been overlooked by the management. Uninformed, we had continued to interact as if nothing was happening while in actuality a part of the roof had burned.

An hour or so later when I was back at the office, I joked with the rehabilitation counselor about keeping our cool under fire. At the same time I realized that, joking aside, it is what you do not know that can harm you.

chapter 68

Scars

*I*heard the shrill cry. It was ear piercing, the kind of sound a badly hurt animal might make.

"Why don't people take better care of their children!" I thought. It is quite annoying to have to put up with this kind of noise when on vacation and browsing at a beach souvenir shop.

Yet, hardly had I formulated the sentence when I knew something was terribly wrong. My wife, Claire, was calling my name loudly as she came running from the back of the shop to the front. In her arms was our then four-year-old, Tim, bleeding badly and screaming at the top of his lungs.

"Here," she said, handing our son off to me like a football. "Try to stop the bleeding. I'll call for help."

Even though I had been in the Army, the sight of Tim gave me pause. He had stumbled face-first with his mouth open onto the outstretched metal arm of a coat rack with a hook. The force of gravity had carried him down, and as he fell, the long appendage that he had fallen on had penetrated his cheek and torn a large gash in the right side of his mouth from the inside out. A woman handed me a towel. I knew to apply pressure both to stop the bleeding and to cover up the sight of a shocking wound.

When help did not arrive soon, we hustled Tim, our other two sons, and ourselves into what instantly became our Dodge Care-A-Van and headed for the emergency room of the nearest hospital in Myrtle Beach, South Carolina. There Tim and I spent two hours with a plastic surgeon while everyone else waited anxiously. The rest of the summer and early fall were spent in attending to the healing process, which was gradual with less than desired results. Therefore, Tim underwent more procedures and over a year later the scar he had as a result of the accident, although noticeable, was not his most prominent feature.

The trauma and the recovery process I observed and felt as Tim's father are parallel to events in some of our clients' lives. Usually clients come in with psychological rather than physical scars. Yet, the trauma and pain associated with the events that have propelled them to our offices are as real as metal coat racks. They have fallen in some way and been hurt. Recovery takes time and can be frustrating. There are a number of anxious moments. Even when the helping process ends, a residue of unpleasant memories may linger, although more muted or faded. If we and our clients do our work well, these scars will not be the most noticed or noteworthy feature of their lives.

chapter 69

Courtland, the Turkeys, and Me in Knoxville, Tennessee

O ne of the joys of being in counseling is serving the profession as an associational officer. I have done this several times, but at no time has it been any more fun than when I was president of the Association for Counselor Education and Supervision the same year that Dr. Courtland Lee was president of the American Counseling Association. Part of the reason may have to do with contrast. I am a petite (5' 3") White man with a wiry build, whereas Courtland is a tall (6' 3") African American man with a slender build. When we are together, we look like polar opposites, and people tend to stare at us.

As it happened one November afternoon, we both gave brief speeches to the Southern Association for Counselor Education and Supervision in Knoxville, Tennessee. To show gratitude for what we had done, the officers of the association presented each of us with a papier-mâché turkey. The birds were beautifully decorated but were quite large (about the size of basketballs, or "butterballs" in turkey language). Fortunately, they had a wire handle on their bodies by which to carry them, and that made getting them up to our hotel rooms easier. On the way up to the rooms in the elevator, Courtland and I discovered we had the same flight the next day so we decided to catch a taxi together.

Sunday morning came, and we both arrived at the lobby at the same time carrying our bags and turkeys. We hailed a cab and put our suitcases in the trunk while we placed the turkeys in our laps. It was in reaching the airport that the fun really began. Here we were, a short White man and a tall Black man carrying identical papier-mâché turkeys through the lobby of the airport and up to the ticket counter. The personnel behind the desk just smiled, checked our luggage, and told us that if we wanted to keep our turkeys in one piece we would have to carry them on the plane. They also told us our flight was located at the farthest gate from the ticket counter.

So we proceeded to walk together holding our turkeys as they bobbed along on their wire hangers. I felt at times as if we were on a platform stage in Atlantic City like they have for the Miss America contest, and that people were watching us both intensely and in disbelief. Regardless,

I think we brought some real humor to those we passed. I know the memory of our turkey walk continues to this day as does our friendship. Counseling is inclusive. It encompasses a variety of people (and sometimes birds of a different feather) who interact, learn, and have good times together.

chapter 70

Parenthood

$\mathcal{P}$arenthood *can* change your life. I emphasize the word "can" because it does not have to change your life. It depends on whether you really planned to be a parent or parent figure, what you invest in it if it happens to you, and how much you care for children whether they are yours or not.

When I married I was 40. My spouse, Claire, was 35. While we were not ancient, we did feel a lot like the biblical characters Abraham and Sarah because our union was way later than most of our friends. Furthermore, there was real doubt about whether we could have children. Unlike the elderly patriarch and matriarch just referred to, we had not been promised descendants as numerous as the stars in the evening sky or as plentiful as grains of sand on the beach. So, we thought we would try to fulfill our dream but we would accept what happened. There were no guarantees.

Well, we might as well have been living in the "fertile crescent" of the Near East. Claire got pregnant within a couple of months of our marriage. Ben was born the April following our May wedding. Eighteen months later, Nate came, followed by Tim 20 some months afterwards. Thus, in five years we had three children. It was funny in some ways for during this time, the rhythm of our lives seemed to be that we would move, I'd write a book, and we would have a baby. In response to the pattern, Claire finally said after the birth of Tim, "We're not moving again!"

We haven't and we have not had any more children either!

How have children changed us? Well, in various ways. We have both become more sensitive to the plights of children (not just our own). We have realized that a grown person can survive sleep deprivation and still keep a sense of humor. For instance, after one sleepless night, when I got ready to go to work, all Claire could do was smile and say, "Looks like you dressed yourself" (which was true as I had different colored shoes on my feet and a tie around my neck that did not match anything else I was wearing).

Parenthood has also brought home the fact that less time with one's spouse is often stressful and the reality that some situations are unsolvable. Acting childlike but not childish is another lesson I have learned. Then there is the realization that clichés my spouse and I heard growing up, such as "Because I said so," are phrases we have sometimes been guilty of repeating to our children. Hundreds of words dealing with human relationships such as "modeling," "volunteering," "learning," "understanding," "trying," "sighing," "reliving," "forgetting," and "forgiving" are now at the forefront of my vocabulary. They live on the tip of my tongue when I describe what happened starting in 1986. These words were in the background before.

Whether we have naturally born children in our lives, adopt children, become foster parents/grandparents, Big Brothers, Big Sisters, or we just relate to children because we love, value, and want to help them, we are all parents. Some of us may have more fiduciary responsibilities but ultimately we all, in some ways, rear the next generation. I am sure Abraham and Sarah knew that. Parenthood is not about age, numbers, or biology. It is about obligation, dedication, and caring in the best and worst of times for those who are young and need our guidance. Having committed to a course of action and become immersed in it, such as caring for a child, we can never be the same again, nor should we.

Points to Ponder

1. What have you learned from good colleagues and friends that continues to be of value to you?

2. What have you learned about yourself in times of failure or despair? How do you use that knowledge now?

3. How have chance encounters influenced your development or friendships? Be specific.

WORKING WITH GROUPS AND FAMILIES

Emotions ricochet around the group
fired by an act of self-disclosure
in an atmosphere of trust.
I, struck by the process,
watch as feelings penetrate the minds
of involved members
and touch off new reactions.
Change comes from many directions
triggered by simple words.

—Gladding, 1999[8]

Some of the most trying and rewarding experiences we can have in counseling come when we do therapeutic work with groups and families. The dynamics differ dramatically in these situations as opposed to those when counseling is delivered on a one-to-one basis. Working with groups and families can be a bit bizarre and/or humorous, such as in this section's vignettes on "Sex Therapy: The Challenge" and "Humor." Likewise, experiences with these populations can be dramatic and enlightening, such as in the stories here on "Three's a Crowd But Four's a Family Counseling Session" and "Drama Break."

Regardless of the immediate impact, it is crucial that we as counselors work with groups and families. Not only is such an arrangement more economical for clients, but it may be more significant in the long run because few clients live outside the influence of these groups in their everyday lives.

chapter 71

The Other Side of Labels

One of my most memorable experiences as a counselor was in working with a schizophrenic man in a group. I was relatively new to the counseling profession and inexperienced at running groups. The man was a veteran of mental health services and had gone through a number of psychiatrists, psychologists, counselors, social workers, and nurses before he got to me. Like a tidal wave on a beach, he was pretty overwhelming. I was not sure what to do with him. I sensed he did not expect a moment's trouble from me. A few words, a little action, and I too would probably give up on him. He would "win," having defeated another clinician again.

However, I did not do what he expected because I really did not know how. I kept treating him with respect; I did not follow him out of the room when he would get upset in the group. I always thanked him for his input.

One day he could not stand it any longer. He said to me, "Where did you go to school, and did you really learn anything about mental health services there?" Before I could reply, he went on with a statement, "You don't know how to work with schizophrenics. Listen, I'm schizophrenic. Everybody tells me that, and I've tried to show you. You're never going to make it in this profession unless you learn to become agitated instead of treating me like a normal person."

"Oh," I replied. "Wouldn't it be easier if you tried something new? I mean, I'm not a quick study, and there must be something you wish to do besides what you're doing."

He looked puzzled, but he stayed in the group that day. To my surprise, as the group went on, he began telling the other members about some land he had seen near his family's farm that he would like to work. One thing led to another, and his hope turned into plans and finally action as he began to make a transition.

The point is that through discussing who he was in the group he discovered another side of himself that was healthier than he expected. That self was able to grow in the "we-ness" that was the group. As far as I know, he is still on the land he purchased and a part of a productive community.

chapter 72

The Power of Nancy Drew

*T*he power of literature struck me a few years ago when I was working with a group of adolescents. In the group was a young woman who wanted to be recognized for her independence and ability. As the group went on I asked her, "Who do you know who is like you want to be?"

To my surprise she said, "Nancy Drew."

"Oh," I replied. "What is it about Miss Drew that makes her attractive to you?"

To which she stated, "Nancy can think for herself. She is courageous, and she is just as smart and able as any boy."

From then on when the young woman would talk about what she wished to achieve, a group member would always ask, "How would Nancy Drew do it?"

"Like this," the young woman would reply as she enacted positive behaviors before all assembled.

chapter | 73

Airtime

*E*veryone needs air in order to survive. Participants in a group need "air" in order to thrive. Let me explain.

By *air* in a group I am not referring to the gaseous mixture of elements surrounding the earth that all of us breathe. Rather, I am referring to the amount of time a person gets to speak in a group. Group members learn from each other both directly and vicariously. In order to learn best, however, they need to have time to give a voice to what they have processed externally and internally. Some need more time to *air* than others, but everyone needs to be heard.

Even in groups that are primarily task or educationally related, members do best when they are empowered to speak and when they realize their voice is valued. In such cases, they take "ownership" of the group and contribute more to it.

By obtaining input at the beginning of each group, for example through "go-rounds" (where every member gets a chance to talk), the group progresses. It is like one member told me after I solicited information from him:

"When I speak I feel as if I'm not just another person who fills a chair. I think when you and others ask me for an opinion, you really care. That makes me feel alive."

chapter 74

Three's a Crowd But Four's a Family Counseling Session

For some families who come to counseling, there is a lack of trying by family members, and the result is a trying experience. A vivid memory I have of resistance to change came when I once saw a family that was supposed to be composed of four people. As I greeted the family, I noticed only three people.

"I'm a bit confused," I said. "I see that you report that you are a family of four, but I count only three noses. Since I assume there is a nose connected with each person, it appears to me that we are a person short."

"That would be Eleanor," said the mother. "We call her the 'Wild Thing.' She's in the car but refuses to come in."

"How big is Eleanor?" I asked.

"About 98 pounds," said the father. "She's 13 years old."

"Well," I replied. "Go get Eleanor and bring her into the session. I am charging you, and the clock is running. We won't start the session without her."

The protests were great.

"She'll scratch our eyes out," said her brother.

"She'll never speak to us again," groaned the mother.

"She'll never let us come back," sighed the father.

"Go get her," I repeated.

Thus, they reluctantly went out to the parking lot. What occurred next was not a pretty sight. There was a bit of a struggle and a few raised voices, but with the odds at 3 to 1, about 10 minutes later Eleanor was brought into my office with her parents and brother carrying her like a captured wild animal.

I interacted with the family, including Eleanor, the rest of the session. We focused on how to tame the wildness going on in the family. Eleanor actually offered some good suggestions. However, the important part of the therapeutic work started with a change in the family's interaction with their scapegoated daughter. The parents had taken some control over a situation about which they had previously felt helpless and angry. The bringing in of Eleanor brought the family into dealing with issues that were separating them. There was no magic to the process—

only a struggle, which is a common denominator in almost every productive therapeutic encounter. However, there was change that years later resulted in visits, hugs, phone calls, and mail that kept the family together even with time, aging, marriages, newborns, and death.

chapter 75

Sex Therapy: The Challenge

*A*young couple I once saw had two difficulties: They had sexual problems and were mentally challenged. I was not married and was somewhat reluctant to work with them because of this personal circumstance. However, my supervisor told me that he thought I was no more limited than the couple, so (taking that as a compliment) I agreed to work with them. In order to do the best job possible I thought it important to study sex manuals and be familiar with body parts and functions. Therefore, I checked out a bevy of books and studied late into the night for several evenings to my delight and edification.

Then I went into the session with great anatomical information and the intent to find out exactly what the problem was and resolve it.

"What brings you here?" I inquired.

"A 1986 Ford pickup" was the answer I received.

Undaunted, I then asked both people in my best clinical voice what was of most concern to them sexually. I received only vague and convoluted answers in regard to the specifics about which I was inquiring. Finally frustrated, I tried a concrete approach and said, "Tell me this. Just how far have you two gone?"

To that the young woman looked at her husband curiously and he at her. Then she looked at me and replied in a rather matter-of-fact manner, "Well, we've gone about as far as Atlanta."

From her response (which was much more literal than I wanted), I realized that competency and change are interrelated. If counseling is to be meaningful, a simple and unconfused language must be used. Furthermore, I found out that pertinent questions asked in the wrong way will get responses that are unbelievably off the mark.

chapter 76

Drama Break

$\mathcal{S}$ ometimes people need a break in the way they relate to one another. Such a break creates opportunities. I first realized this fact while working with a dysfunctional couple. He was a construction worker, massive in size but slow in speech. She was a secretary, speedy in her clerical skills and fast with her opinions. The trouble was that when they would argue, she would begin to outtalk him. In frustration and anger, he would grab her arm and twist it around her back until she was quiet. (I used to call them the "twist and shout" couple after one of my favorite songs from the 1960s by the Righteous Brothers. However, there was nothing melodious about their relationship.)

One day they came in to see me, and the pattern started again. Just like Bob Dylan used to sing that you do not have to be a weatherman to know which way the wind blows, I realized that one need not be a family counselor to see the gathering storm of conflict emerging within a relationship. Thus, rather than wait for the thunder and lightning of what was to come, I asked the couple to freeze in their tracks as if a gust of cold arctic air had just swept over them. (This type of action was not too hard for any of us to imagine because each winter strong cold fronts frequently swept into the state of Connecticut in which we lived.)

After they froze in place, I told them we were going to act out a scene. The man was to play himself and express his concerns but speak in a slower than normal voice. The woman was to act just the opposite of her usual behavior. She was simply to listen. As she did, she was to pick up on his words as she might pick up on dictation, and she was to read his body cues in addition to understanding his language. Then she was to give her husband feedback about what she heard and saw. With that explained, I then shouted, "Action!"

They performed well and talked about the event at some length after I yelled, "Cut!" Then we reversed the roles. Although there was no camera or lights, insight and understanding emerged from these staged dramatic moments. Had we not stopped for some drama, the situation might have stayed the same or deteriorated. However, a new sense of timing led to new understanding and more productive ways of interacting. Some weeks later, I actually saw the couple at a concert together looking as if they were really enjoying themselves as they danced to some upbeat music on the grass to the tune by which I had described them earlier: "Twist and Shout."

chapter 77

An Unexpected Reconciliation: Laura Ashley

f all the couples I have ever seen in my professional career, this one initially seemed the "most hopeless." She came from a wealthy and sophisticated background. He called her "Laura Ashley"—the name on her well-tailored clothes and accessories. He came from poverty and was crude in manner, dress, and speech. He loved to hunt, fish, and drink beer with the boys. She called him "Billy Bob." He went from one manual labor job to another and liked the freedom it afforded him.

I wondered how they had ever found each other—much less me. I could imagine the initial excitement and attraction they had for one another because of their differences. However, I could not imagine that they would have carried their relationship all the way to the altar, tied the knot, and had a child two years later. Now in their 10th year of marriage, they sat before me. She complained that he was "uninteresting" and "boorish." He said she was too concerned with the little and unimportant things of life like her looks. "Why do you shop at those expensive stores?" he inquired.

"If ever there was a match not meant to be this is probably it," I thought. Thus, I was not surprised that she called after the first session and canceled the second.

"There is no use talking about our marriage," she said. "The writing is on the wall, and it reads 'Go directly to court and divorce.'"

I did not argue with her and thought that like so many couples I had seen in marriage counseling, this one came too late to get help.

What did surprise me was a call from him.

"I want to see you," he said. "I want to save our relationship."

I could have brushed him off and have put up a strong argument for him not coming for counseling, but he seemed so sincere that I agreed. A few days later he showed up, and we began what was the start of a long-term therapeutic relationship. I was truly amazed that he came each week. He passionately talked about "Laura Ashley," but I thought it was futile. How could he do anything to win her back?

"Tigers don't change their stripes," I once said to him.

"This tiger does," he responded.

So, he did. He was committed. He went back to school, changed careers, started working out, began reading books from *The New York Times* best-seller list, and even found a church to attend. I do not think I have ever seen anyone work harder for anything in my life. He showed up promptly for each of our appointments, too, and threw himself into our sessions. Rather than demand, he invited Laura Ashley to give him another try. On the fifth request, she consented to see him, and after that I began seeing them together. They made it back as a couple to my surprise. As they were leaving my office for the last time, he turned around and said, "From now on, please call me William."

Sometimes we, as counselors, work hard to promote change. The best times are when our clients do.

chapter 78

Humor

Counseling is never a joke, but it does require a sense of humor and there is often levity in it. Clients laugh more as they get better. Life is not so grave and serious. There is a connection, a positive correlation, between having some laughter in one's life and being able to deal effectively with reality. For example, when a young promiscuous woman I was working with improved, she smiled broadly when I said that the way she could stay out of trouble from now on was by remembering two words: "No. No."

Paul Watzlawick has pointed out that in life some situations are "hopeless but not serious" as well as "serious but not hopeless." Humor comes into play in those situations in which clients come to counseling feeling hopeless, especially if their situation is not serious; that is, easily solvable. For instance, I once saw a couple in which each person was upset over the behavior of the other to be either orderly or sloppy. Friction in their lives revolved around how they would keep their house. One wanted everything neat; the other wanted everything casual. The breakthrough in their relationship (as opposed to the breakup of it) came when they agreed they would maintain both kinds of rooms. For example, the living room was formal, but the bedroom was bohemian. When they saw the folly of what they had been fighting about and how relatively simple it was to solve, they laughed.

Clients are sometimes like a math book, full of problems. But as counselors we need to be solution-focused. Along with other clinical skills in such a process, humor helps us move from the unsolvable to the possible. Humor assists us in keeping our sanity and humanity while our clients work out ways to live life more fully.

chapter 79

Research and a Reframe Within the Family

Sometimes we can get too caught up in our professional lives. That fact was brought home to me literally in my home by my wife. I came to her one day enthusiastic about some research I had recently read. The article that had caught my attention was on marital happiness. It stated that a couple's degree of happiness decreased with each child they had. Claire, my wife, who was pregnant at the time with our third child and feeling queasy and tired with two toddlers underfoot, seemed nonplussed by my remarks. She even appeared to become a little annoyed as I droned on with some excitement about what I had found. By the time I had finished expounding on the implications of the work I had absorbed, I could tell she did not want to hear any more. Thus, I went back to my office and further study.

A couple of months later the blessed event we had waited for, Tim, arrived. It was a chilly March night, but the cold had no impact on the delivery. However, the previous conversation Claire and I had had about marital happiness was not finished. In recovery, with our new son close by her side, she looked up at me from the bed and said, "The honeymoon's not over. There are just more people on it."

Sure enough, she was right. Although more stressed than ever before, we have more fun than previously because of the way we now interact with our children and each other. Claire's reframe on the situation changed the perspective we had as a couple without cooling my enthusiasm to read the research. It gave us the best of both worlds.

chapter 80

Words Alone

*I*f you pay attention to words alone, you may find yourself alone and lonely, having failed to make an intervention that would be helpful. For instance, in working with a couple who had been a cantankerous duo together longer than I had been alive, whom I shall call the Bickersons, I realized I was doomed if I stayed with their verbal content. From the minute the couple arrived, they were at each other verbally. In fact, they were quite good at their word attacks. She would hit him with a barb, and he would jab back with an insult. Then she would land a demeaning comment squarely on his chin, and he would stagger but counterpunch with a discounting statement of his own. Back and forth, they went at it for about five minutes, flipping words as if they were flapjacks, until having demonstrated their potency, they stopped and turned to me, and the husband said (almost smugly, as if flipping me a hot one off the grill), "So what are you going to do to help us?"

My blood was flowing like warm maple syrup, and my mind was racing in time with the words that had been let loose. I realized that instead of interacting in their arena I needed to change the scene if I was to avoid being fried, grilled, or burned. So, I replied, "I'm sending you to your corners. That's the end of Round 1."

Thus, before you could say "Muhammad Ali," I got them on their feet and directed each to go to a separate corner of the office as if they were in a boxing ring and not cooking in the kitchen. Then I clapped my hands together and said, "Come out and sit down; it's Round 2." They did but were somewhat stunned. They had entered a new domain and a new way of seeing and being. The system they were used to fighting in had changed. In their new environment, well-worn ways of interacting were not allowed. New and productive ways of trying to relate were taught, tried, and modified. Everyone won.

Points to Ponder

1. Who are some people, either fictional or real, after whom you model your life? What characteristics do they have that you would like to emulate?

2. When did someone make a change you did not expect? How did that make you feel? What was the outcome of the change?

3. What do you find humorous? Think about a funny event in your family or a group and what made it so.

PROFESSIONAL DEVELOPMENT

I remember doing role plays in your class
trying to look cool, while my palms sweated
and my heart beat as fast as a hummingbird's wing.
You were supportive ... giving me feedback
while encouraging me to explore
the universe that was myself.
Other classes, other seasons came as quickly
as the sound of laughter and as silently as sorrow.
With you I traveled the roads to conventions
sharing all the light and darkness of the time that came to be.

—Gladding, 1989[9]

*A*s professional counselors we either develop or stagnate. The half-life of knowledge is decreasing yearly, and the counselor who does not actively keep up will by default fall behind and become obsolete. Continuing education and supervision are two important ways of combatting irrelevance and obsolescence.

The vignettes in this section highlight that fact along with the importance of counselors learning how the legal system works in regard to clients. Research and learning from others are also stressed. Planned movement in a growth-producing direction does not always meet with success, but it usually results in knowledge that is enabling.

chapter 81

Supervision

$\mathcal{S}$upervision is a multidimensional process that helps counselors keep their skills current and potent. It is a learning experience that is essential for both novice and experienced clinicians.

When I initially became a counselor, I opted for supervision that was more didactic and instructive. However, over the years I have come to value and use peer supervision more. In such an atmosphere, growth occurs through input of fellow counselors and dialogue with them.

For instance, I remember being stuck as to some ways I could communicate the importance of a couple getting help for their daughter. A direct, rational approach had not worked. Then one of my fellow supervisors asked, "How do your clients get to your office?"

"There are many ways for them to get there," I replied.

"What does that tell you about your predicament?" was his response.

Indeed, the more I thought about it, the more I realized I could open up avenues for my clients to travel by having the couple "look down the road" of the options they had for their daughter. In the next session, I opened up with the road metaphor and instead of suggesting, I let my clients tell and sell me some possibilities for obtaining assistance. They found some options that were realistic and pragmatic. They even followed through on a couple of their better ideas and literally got somewhere. As a result, they were happier, I was less stressed, and the counseling was successful.

Supervision improves our abilities to see and be with our clients and to improve our clinical skills. It is sometimes direct, but often it is reflective. It is a powerful way to overcome resistance that sometimes inadvertently is our own.

chapter 82

Court: The Rules of the Game

*T*he first time I went to court as a counselor I went with a hope and a prayer. I should have gone prepared.

I assumed that a court of law was a place where all you had to do was "tell the truth, the whole truth, so help you God" and all would work out well. I was unaware of the rules of the games that attorneys play.

For instance, my attorney approached me like a warm teddy bear and pitched questions to me that could only be characterized as "softballs." "What was my name?" "What were my degrees?" "How had I handled the client in question?" When the questions were over, I felt like I had hit home runs every time I had come up to bat.

In contrast, the opposing attorney rushed toward me with all the characteristics of a grizzly bear. He bore down with queries that were a mixture of fastballs, curves, and sliders. The game had changed. We were playing "hardball." "Was my clinical degree from a nationally ranked program?" "What percentage of counselors would have done exactly what I did in regard to the client?" "Did I feel any sexual attraction to the client?" (That one my attorney objected to, as did I.) The long and short of what happened, however, was that after the cross-examination was over, I understood the Spanish Inquisition much better. I also knew what it was like to "strike out" . . . repeatedly.

I have not been to court a lot since that first encounter. However, I have never gone without consulting an attorney and colleagues beforehand. The rules of the game are different, and to enter without an understanding is to invite a mauling.

chapter 83

Research and Theory:
A Reminder From Carl Rogers

*W*hen I began my career, many of the pioneers of counseling were at their zenith. Therefore, I listened to lectures by Carl Rogers, Gilbert Wrenn, Albert Ellis, B. F. Skinner, Virginia Satir, and Carl Whitaker, among others. I even took a four-week course at the New School in New York City with Rollo May. Because I received a lot of firsthand information from these individuals, I thought I was in a position to critique their work or at least compare and contrast their approaches. I did so in the classes I was teaching. Then one day I thought I would put one of my lectures in the form of an article and send it off for publication. I wrote a comparison between Heinz Kohut and Carl Rogers. It was published in the *Journal of Counseling & Development* in 1986. I felt good, and proudly showed this pithy but what I considered profound contribution to the professional literature to any colleague I could trap in between classes.

Later, a letter came. It had a California return address. I knew instinctively who had sent it. Carl Rogers had read my article. He was now giving me his opinions. With nervous hands, I tremblingly opened the envelope and delicately unfolded the stationery within it. Sure enough, it was from Rogers. However, instead of giving me new ideas, he gave me a piece of his mind. How could I compare him and his theory with Kohut and his object relations hypothesis? As Rogers pointed out, he had tested his ideas and they were research-based. Kohut's thoughts were just that—thoughts! He had no empirical proof for his proposals.

I was surprised at the words from Rogers. They were stern. The unconditionally accepting man had drawn a line in the sand and basically told me not to cross it again. If I did, I knew I could be assured of at least another letter. At first, my feelings vacillated. I was sure that my opinions had merit. However, as I contemplated the epistle, I began to realize Carl Rogers had a reason for addressing me the way he did. He had given his life to building his theory, and the reputation of his person and his work depended on how what he had written was interpreted. The two approaches I had focused on had entirely different research bases, and Rogers wanted to let me know his ideas had been empirically tested.

It was a teachable moment. Since then I have tried in my own work to be more careful in what I compare and how. I also read the literature with a bit more of a critical eye. Corrective feedback, even when blunt and unwelcome, can make a positive difference in the way we live and the way we look at research and theory.

chapter 84

My Pal Sal

hen I became a counselor, I knew something about individual and group therapy but nothing about how to work with families. I assumed that I could use the skills I had refined with individuals and groups on families until I met my first family. Then I realized that reflection, "I" statements, and even confrontation were not the same when applied in such an environment.

Fortunately, within my counseling setting was a colleague who had received family therapy training at the Philadelphia Child Guidance Clinic. He offered to mentor and teach me how to work with families. However, he had one condition.

"Before I see a family with you," he stated simply, "I want you to read some books by Sal Minuchin."

Eager to make a good impression on him and to learn as much as I could, I said I would.

"But tell me," I said, "what has she written?"

My colleague looked at me in disbelief but said kindly, "'Sal' is an abbreviation for Salvador. I'll bring you a list of his texts tomorrow."

So I began my immersion into a field, family counseling, I have come to love. If my mentor had been overly sensitive or insulted by my ignorance, I would not have advanced in my knowledge. However, I was allowed to make mistakes and learn from them. Sometimes we as counselors need to remember that a mistake is not the worse thing that can happen to us or our clients. Such occasions provide educational opportunities if we stay non-defensive, open, and willing to learn from them.

chapter 85

Adjectives and Adverbs

*A*s counselors we are sought out for a number of reasons. As a group we are good listeners and problem solvers, often with even temperaments. Therefore, individuals in responsible positions seek us out for consultation and even employment in areas outside of counseling.

During one part of my career, I served the president of Wake Forest University as his assistant. Although there was no formal job description, I basically handled most of the toxic situations coming into the office, such as irritated constituents, upset parents, and overwrought faculty and students. I also drafted much of the university's official correspondence.

After a year on the job, I had my first review.

"How am I doing?" I inquired, stealing a line from Ed Koch, the mayor of New York during the 1980s.

"Fine" was the answer from a man who was fairly brief in giving praise. "There is only one thing I want you to work on."

"Oh," I replied.

"Yes," the CEO of the institution said. "Cut back on the use of adjectives."

"Okay," I responded and the interview ended.

All seemed to go well for a second year and at the end of it, I went in again for my evaluation.

"How am I doing?" I queried again, thinking it had worked well for me once and that it just might again.

"Fine" was the answer. "There is just one thing I want you to work on."

"Oh," I replied. "What's that?"

"Cut out using adverbs" was the response.

"Okay," I said, realizing that now I had lost the use of two primary ways of expressing myself.

When I went home and told my wife about the encounter, all she could say was, "What next? Gerunds? Participles?"

Well, I am happy to report that after eliminating adjectives and adverbs, I was not asked to refrain from using other parts of speech. I am also pleased to say I learned something that has helped me as a counselor, too. I find now that in working with clients I am less prone to use adjectives and adverbs unless they are needed. For instance, I tend to say something like "You are troubled" rather than "You are very troubled."

Sometimes we need to employ all of the verbal abilities we have in order to make the most direct impact on the persons with whom we work. In other situations, less is more. I think of this maxim often. I think it makes me a better counselor and more sensitive to meeting the needs of those I serve.

chapter 86

A Quiet Riot: Life as an Oxymoron

*T*here are certain words I love such as *juxtaposition, alliteration,* and yes, *oxymoron.* When I think of who I am, I realize that I may be more of an oxymoron than not. On the outside, I am calm. Inside, there is much activity. You might say I am a quiet riot.

I'm not alone in having this distinction. I think many of my clients are the same. They appear one way externally and yet internally they are totally different. The bully or the oppositional defiant child is most likely insecure inside. Yet, you would never know it from observing his or her behavior. Likewise, the shy retiring person who is hesitant to make eye contact may well be experiencing constant internal dialogue about what he or she should do and when. I often think of those who are old and frail in the same way. On the surface they do not say or do a great deal. However, inside they may well be churning with memories and wishes.

Thus, one of the things I seek to do as both a professional and a person is to realize that life goes on well below the surface of what we see. While congruence is valued and manifests itself in both external and internal dimensions of a person coming together, the fact is that many people, especially those who seek counseling services, are not congruent. And even though we may strive for such a state, often we as counselors lack togetherness. Being a "quiet riot" or any other seemingly contradictory state is not too unusual. In fact, it may be the norm. Hopefully though, through counseling, meditation, and other means we can find balance and a peace within as well as without.

chapter 87

Thunder, Turmoil, and Thoughts

*I*t had been a difficult day. My schedule had been jam-packed with a host of new clients who had some serious problems. To make it even more harried in the midst of the hurriedness, a series of storms had rolled through the area and played havoc with the electrical system. Therefore, there was turbulence both inside and outside my working environment. I wondered if my clients had been as disturbed by the disruptive atmosphere as I had. Rain was one thing; the chaos of a passing weather system was another.

I can still remember the bitter taste of almost-cold coffee that I consumed twice that day with the hope that the dark liquid I poured from the pot would contain something hot. Both my taste buds and I had been disappointed. I can also still see the streak of lightning that grounded nearby and hear the crackle of an oak tree across the street that was split in two as a result of a direct hit. (I have actually wondered since if the violent storm so pivotal in the life of Martin Luther was of this nature. If so, I understand the non-*DSM* term *conversion reactions* in new ways.)

Now it was late in the afternoon—time for paperwork and the updating of charts. Time for reflection and attention to making sure I was documenting what I had done. The last session I had conducted had been particularly rough. The woman who was my client had been demanding. She wanted everything fixed now, and there was no reasoning with her. I could see why she was seeking treatment, but I thought after we finished working that I might need a good counselor too, if for nothing more than catharsis. After all, I was reading about primal scream therapy then. I could be a case of one, I thought, in a qualitative research experiment to see if such a release really was effective.

So I was glad for a break from the rush and fuss of the preceding events. However, as I was dutifully writing out clinical notes, a procedure that was routine and somewhat mundane, I found myself jotting down something different than usual. Instead of the prosaic, pathological, and intervention language I normally transcribed onto an 8-1/2" by 11" yellow sheet of paper, I found new thoughts—poetic words were rhythmically flowing from my pen. It was almost as if they were demanding a life of their own outside the confines of my mind. I had the power to make their appearance possible and positive, or I could simply ignore them. I chose the former course because I must admit I was charged up already and excited to see where the process would go.

I had been working as a counselor for only a couple of years when this occurred, and this incident was not the first time I had had other than clinical words come to mind. However, this occasion was the first time I openly entertained the thoughts and emotions that accompanied poetic words. Thus, as the sunlight peaked through the clouds and played in the red and orange maple leaves outside my window, I wrote down the following sentences:

> *In the midst of a day that has brought mainly gray skies,*
> *Hard rain, and two cups of lukewarm coffee*
> *You come to me with Disney wishes*
> *Wanting me to change into*
> *A Houdini figure, with Daniel Boone's style,*
> *Prince Charming's grace, and Abe Lincoln's wisdom,*
> *Who with magic words, a special wand, frontier spirit,*
> *and perhaps a smile*
> *Can cure all trouble in a flash.*
> *But reality sits in a green cushioned chair, lightning*
> *has struck a nearby tree,*
> *Yesterday ended another month, I'm uncomfortable sometimes*
> *in silence,*
> *And unlike fantasy figures, I can't always be what you see in*
> *your mind.*

To say that the writing of the words was transforming may be to overstate the case. However, I realized something fresh in the process of writing. I was calmer, and I had insight into my day and especially into the last session I had had. My graduate education had not prepared me for such an event, but then my professors had said counselor training was a lifelong event—not a sentence of two or three years. So, I thought, here is a lesson.

Counseling is an art as well as a science. We who are in the profession as practitioners, teachers, and supervisors need to pay attention to that artistic side of our discipline as well as the artistic side of ourselves if we are to be complete and competent. Unless we do, we will be mechanical and in the long run less than our best.

chapter 88

Who Wants To Work?

*W*hen my son Nate was eight years old, he informed me that he was learning the countries of South America just for the fun of it. After listening to him rattle off a few, I said, "Why not learn the countries of Africa?"

He replied, "There are too many. That wouldn't be fun; it'd be work."

Sometimes the number of factors that our clients face seems overwhelming. However, if we can help them clarify their visions, they are more likely to work toward realistic achievements. In the process, they are likely to become more connected with their friends, themselves, and their inner resources. They are also more likely to be productive in counseling. Some situations are simpler to deal with than others, like memorizing the names of countries in South America. Others require what Nate would describe as "African effort," that is, a focused dedication to the task at hand.

Regardless, I never ask clients in any setting what they want to talk about. Rather, I ask them what they want to work on. The emphasis of such phrasing may be subtle, but the outcome can be significant.

chapter 89

Not by Work Alone

_E_arly in my career, I devoted almost all of my time to either counseling or writing about counseling. I was intense, and the payoff was publications. However, there was something missing. I realized the missing link when I went for an important job interview at a rather high-profile university as a counselor educator.

All went well until I had my interview with the dean of the school, who was pleasant but firm. He looked at my resumé and in a rather serious tone said, "I see you write a lot. There are a lot of publications here."

"Yes," I said (with a sense of pride). "I find it therapeutic."

Without missing a beat, he then said, "You must be very sick."

At the time I probably was sick, at least in a couple of ways. I was sick in the realization that this particular interview was virtually over and that the dean before me had recognized I was on the fast track to burnout because I was not doing anything outside the profession. I was also sick in that I was over-focused on my work instead of my overall life.

Just as we do not live by bread alone, living only to be a counselor or a writer may not be the healthiest thing to do. We need to think avocationally as well as vocationally. That means making time in our day for what I call the 4Fs of life outside of work: family, friends, fitness, and fun. Since that interview I have taken the time to play games, relax at the pool, go on vacations, and talk more with those I am closest to outside of my family as well as my wife and children. It has been enriching and rewarding. I still write—a lot—but I enjoy it more. I control it rather than it controlling me.

chapter 90

Rejection

Few sentences in the English language are more frustrating to counselors who write than the words "Thank you for your submission, but we do not find it suitable for publication." The reason why the words are so emotionally devastating is because they are critical and counselors are sensitive. In addition, to be rejected is the antithesis of what counseling is about. Furthermore, a manuscript that is not accepted is work that many counselors look back on as effort that was in vain. They could have been doing something more productive, such as spending time with their family, relaxing with a hobby, or seeing clients. Therefore, they often become sad and despondent. However, I think the opposite reaction is called for. There is a challenge to rejection that calls us to inspect what we are doing, what we are saying, and the way we are conveying it to others.

I once had a manuscript that I thought had potential rejected by a periodical in which I thought readers would enjoy and benefit from reading it. I was downcast at first, but as I reflected on the critical comments, I could see that some were deserved. Therefore, in my spare time, I started cleaning up the manuscript. The next year, I noticed there had been a change in the editor of the journal to which I had submitted. Thus, I sent the revision back and waited. A few months later, a fat envelope with a rejection letter arrived in my mailbox again. I read the comments, put the materials away, and thought. Then, I pulled them out again and once more started to revise. Three years later, the editor of the journal changed again. My manuscript was updated, revised, and resubmitted. The third time was the charm. The reviews were wonderful to read.

Rejection is not the worst thing that can happen to a paper or a person. Giving up is. Although unpleasant, rejection can lead to introspection and change.

chapter 91

Counselors Anonymous

evelopment as a counselor continues after one's formal education has ended. There are seminars to attend on the latest trends
in the field and continuing education experiences to participate
in to hone clinical skills. Outside of these structured ways of professionally improving oneself, there are more informal means by which to grow,
such as discussions with colleagues and even former students.

The never-ending nature of developing as a counselor was dramatically illustrated to me when I was a professor of counselor education at
the University of Alabama at Birmingham. Some recent graduates invited me to join them after work at a local tavern to "talk" counseling.
When I arrived, I found they wanted not only to engage in conversation
but also to induct me into a group they had organized. The group was
called "counselors anonymous" and was unlike any other "anonymous"
organization that I have ever encountered. It was composed of practitioners who saw themselves evolving as the field of counseling grew. It
was not that the individuals in the group were addicted to the profession. Rather, it was that they envisioned themselves becoming stronger
and better as the profession of counseling increased in status and they
improved their skills.

Thus, before this group I pledged to continue to strive to develop and
to identify myself as one of them, that is, a counselor. There was no
secret handshake. There were no papers to sign or membership forms to
fill out. Rather, the only action I took that day was to continue to identify myself with the field of which I was already a part. I have by saying
before every presentation I make: "My name is Sam, and I'm a counselor."

I plan to keep doing this forever. Growing as a counselor is something from which I hope never to recover.

Points to Ponder

1. What has been your experience with supervision? How has it helped you grow?

2. When have you been rejected? How did it feel? What did you do (or wish you had done) to make the experience better?

3. Time is an important commodity. We sometimes take it for granted. In what ways do you use your time to grow personally and professionally? Are there ways you could use your time better?

DEVELOPMENTAL CONSIDERATIONS

When she turned 40
she took it hard
Like breaking an arm
or having a baby.
Awkward, painful, new,
she was hesitant in her moves
unsure of what to do.
Not knowing kept her going
without clear direction.
I met her at the crossroads.

—Gladding, © 2005[10]

Who we are and what we become as people and professionals are frequently tied in with how we face and react to events in our lives, especially the unexpected and unpredictable. Life is both funny and serious, and it is in seeing both sides, sometimes simultaneously, that we gain maturity that allows us to continue to develop.

The vignettes in this section are like those that have preceded them in that they are events as seen through the eyes of clients and a counselor that have made an impression on their lives. The senses of seeing, hearing, and touching particularly come to the forefront in these stories as they do in most incidents in life that we remember. As you read these pieces you may want to examine times in your own life that helped make you more sensitive and alive.

chapter 92

Aging But Not Developing

evelopmental crises demand our attention. Aging, having children, not reaching one's goals at a particular time, or failing to keep up professionally are examples of developmental events that can potentially create a crisis.

I once had a middle-aged woman come into my office who personified the power of stagnation. She was a graduate of what she described as one of the finest counseling programs in the nation. However, she had obtained her master's degree more than 25 years ago and had not opened a book on counseling since. Now she was inquiring as to what she could do with her education.

"Well," I said, "Are you nationally certified?"

She looked at me inquisitively and said, "What's that?"

"Well, certification comes through NBCC," I explained.

"I watch CBS and FOX," she countered.

"No," I replied. "NBCC is not a television station; it is the National Board for Certified Counselors."

"Oh?" she responded. "It wasn't around when I got my degree. I never heard of it."

So, I explained further. "Becoming a nationally certified counselor (NCC) might help you in getting licensed in this state because the test given is the same."

She looked puzzled and said, "I already have a license. I've been driving a long time, and as long as I keep my record clean, I won't have to take the test again."

"No," I said emphatically, realizing she was going to drive me crazy if I let her. "I'm talking about being licensed as a counselor in North Carolina."

"When did that happen?" she inquired in her Rip Van Winkle style.

"1983 was when the initial registration law was enacted," I said, "followed in 1994 with licensure."

"I wasn't that interested in counseling then," she replied.

"Well," I said, "certification and licensure are important if you want to practice as a counselor. Likewise, becoming a member of Chi Sigma Iota would be good."

She seemed to beam at the mention of Chi Sigma Iota.

"I was their sweetheart in college," she said proudly.

"That is Sigma Chi," I countered. "This group does not have a sweetheart that I know of, although if they ever become interested in one, I'll let them know of your availability and experience. You should join because of their emphasis on excellence in counseling."

She smiled, but I could tell she did not give an iota about what I was saying regarding the counseling academic and professional honor society international. Thus, I changed the subject.

"Did you know in our department we have two CACREP-approved programs?" I asked.

Well, as soon as the words were out of my mouth, I wanted to retrieve them. She just stared at me like a deer facing the headlights of an oncoming car, shook her head from side to side, and whispered, "Does CACREP stand for what I think it does?"

And I said, "I don't think so. It is the Council for the Accreditation of Counseling and Related Educational Programs."

Well, the conversation continued going downhill from there. The point is that this graduate of a counseling program had not developed. Rather, she had mentally retired and was completely unaware of the changes and the language that had evolved since she last opened a counseling book. She was developmentally delayed in understanding where the field was, and whether she knew it or not, she was in a crisis because she was ill-informed.

chapter 93

Tree With Lights

I have a friend who took his three-year-old out to choose a Christmas tree. They went to a lot they had visited the year before, but the child did not remember the place or the personnel. Thus, the process of picking out a Christmas tree was new to the child. My friend, in a fatherly type of way, started showing his son the trees from which to pick.

"Mike," he said, as he showed him a fine-looking and affordable tree, "Do you like this tree?"

The boy replied, "Yes."

"Do you want to buy it?" the father then inquired.

The young boy shook his head from side to side and answered, "No."

So they went to another tree, and the father asked again, "Mike, do you like this tree?"

The 3-year-old again answered, "Yes."

"Do you want to buy it?" the father asked hopefully.

Again the same nonverbal response occurred, and the answer was "No."

This scenario went on for a few more trees until the father, somewhat frustrated and now less than filled with the holiday spirit, showed his young son one last tree. To the question of whether he liked the tree, the boy said "yes"; to the question of whether he wanted to buy the tree, the boy again replied, "No."

In exasperation, my friend finally said to his son, "I don't understand. We have seen a lot of trees, and you say that you like them, but you don't want to buy any of them. Tell my why."

The young child looked down for a minute at the ground and then looked up at his father, and with the honesty and innocence of childhood he said, "I was hoping we'd get a Christmas tree with lights."

The boy had not remembered that people put the lights on Christmas trees. All he recalled from age two was that Christmas trees had lights. In his mind, it made sense to get a tree that was decorated. He had a vision of what a Christmas tree should look like, but the vision was uninformed.

Developmental Considerations

The same can be said for some of our clients who become excited after one of our counseling sessions. They have a vision of what their lives should be like. However, for the uninformed the path to achieving their vision is unclear. They do not realize that a dream becomes a reality only through hard work and over time. That is where our job begins.

chapter 94

The Unforgettable New York Adventure

I thought it would just be another family vacation with the excitement of Broadway thrown in as a bonus. Instead it turned out to be a bad scene from a Chevy Chase movie! It all began when my wife, Claire, made reservations for our family of five to go to New York City to see the *Music Man* and stay in downtown Manhattan. It seemed like a culturally enriching event, especially for our three boys. To make the trip even more exciting, she arranged for another couple and their two sons to travel with us.

The drama (and indeed some trauma) began 10 minutes after we got off the plane as our taxi was involved in a three-car crash on the Cross Bronx Freeway. Our youngest son Tim, then age 10, started throwing up after we exited what was left of our cab. Following standard procedures the city's finest called over the EMT crew, which was already on the scene, and before you could say "hog tied," they had strapped Tim to a body board and we headed to the nearest hospital (which happened to be primarily for the indigent). There we spent the next eight hours where Tim, after being unstrapped from the board, had a CAT scan and continued to project his insides outside. Finally, after considerable begging, the medical personnel handling the case made a deal with us for Tim's release. They brought in a large 20-ounce Pepsi in a container about as tall as my son.

"If he can drink this Pepsi and hold it down for an hour, he may go."

At that point, we were desperate. So, I agreed to the deal and wondered if our youngest was up to the task. I need not have speculated. Tim was so weak and exhausted he could barely take a sip. So I quickly realized we would be in our less than luxurious surroundings for days unless I became more proactive, creative, or sneaky. As it turned out, I think I was all three. When the medical personnel left for a few minutes, I took the top off the drink and unashamedly chugged the sweet-tasting soda down my gullet in about 45 seconds as if I was playing "thumper" at a local bar. I then replaced the lid and put the container in Tim's hands. A few minutes later when the doctors and nurses returned they noted (with some surprise) how quickly Tim's drink had been finished. An hour later (after I had made frequent trips to the restroom down the hall), Tim was released and was actually feeling better. He had been sipping water.

By this time, Claire and our other two children had left and made their way to Manhattan. Experienced traveler that I was, I thought I would do the same. When I went to check out and asked where to catch a cab, it dawned on me from the response I received that I might as well have been asking where to catch a cold in the summer.

"Regular taxis do not come here," I was told by the person checking us out. "It is just a little too dangerous."

"Then how do we get to Manhattan?" I inquired.

"Pirate cab," was the reply, and with that my heart fell to my feet. Tim, on the other hand, suddenly perked up. He though we were going to see pirates.

Walking out to the street, I flagged down a pirate cab, although to Tim's chagrin the driver did not have an eye patch or a hat with crossbones. Still, he looked pretty scary and I realized he was looking for loot. On the way to Manhattan and our hotel Tim managed to get sick to his stomach one more time. (It is more blessed to give according to Tim.) I had a handkerchief and cleaned everything up on the plastic-covered seats so that I could feel a bit of an outrage when I realized how much the fare was. I was not disappointed. The pirate cab earned its name that day.

The next morning, we went sightseeing at NBC Studios. Actually, the couple we were with took our two oldest boys with them about an hour ahead of Claire, Tim, and me. Just when we arrived at NBC, proud as peacocks, and were safely in the studios, the anthrax scare began. We were ordered to quickly abandon the building, so we headed out to Rockefeller Plaza and clustered in an extended family group.

Unfortunately, just as we got outside, the husband of the couple we were with started to faint (because of an irregular heart rhythm). He slowly went down right in my arms and I wondered what would happen next. I need not have. "Click. Click. Click." It was the sound of cameras as the paparazzi closed in, not caring about the cause of the fall but concentrating on capturing the moment as if the free world depended on it. I seldom swear, but if I had that day, I would have sworn the photographers who swarmed around us owned stock in Kodak, Nikon, and Fuji.

But my task was to help the man in my arms so I rushed back into the NBC Commissary, bought a $5.00 bottle of water, and talked my way out of the building by telling the security guard that I was immune to anthrax, aphids, and autumn allergies. Somehow it all worked. Our friend was revived and I and a host of onlookers were relieved as the EMT came and took him for a checkup at Bellevue Hospital.

At the end of the day, our family's picture ended up as part of a crowd in Rockefeller Plaza in an issue of *Newsweek* while Claire's picture (holding onto one of the sons of the man who fainted) made the front cover (above and below the fold) in an issue of *The Globe and Mail* (Canada's national newspaper).

More normal events of the long weekend included seeing *The Music Man*, riding to the top of the Empire State Building, and taking a Circle Line Cruise. Our souvenirs included bumps, bruises, scrapes, sprains, a number of pictures, a few toys, and an unbelievable story.

The events made me realize anew the fragile nature of life and how quickly life can change. In retrospect, we were fortunate. Instead of experiencing absurdity, our adventure could have ended in tragedy. The fine line between events in life is thin. To act as if there was all the time in the world is to behave and believe foolishly. As my father used to say when I would putz around, "Sam, you can't be a promising young man forever!"

Thus, if I could give one gift to my clients, it would be to remind them that life takes unexpected turns even when you have it well planned. There is no assurance of where time will take you.

chapter 95

Don't Take It Literally

lients can be quite concrete. That is not necessarily bad, but there is a price to be paid if they are too concrete. In most cases it involves their talking about specifics that have nothing to do with their overall life. Even worse, actions can take place that are a bit bizarre. The latter happened to me once when I was working with a client who was back from the regional mental hospital. My task was to evaluate the client to see if he was ready to readjust to the outside world. However, no one instructed me how I was to complete this task. Instead, I was told, "You're smart. You'll figure it out."

Well, it was nice to think that others thought I was capable, but when the time came for the evaluation, I was still wondering what I was going to do. As I entered the waiting room, however, I got an idea by noticing the number of people in the room who were paging through magazines.

"That's it," I said to myself. "I will grab a few magazines. We will then look at the pictures together, and I will have my client tell me stories about himself related to the pictures."

So I gathered some magazines, put them under my arm, and went back to the office with the client. We then started going through the pages after I gave him the following instructions.

"Clyde," I said, "we're going to look at some pictures in these magazines. I want you to tell me about what you see and how it relates to you."

"Okay" was his response.

The first picture was of a house. He related that he lived in one and that it was made of wood.

"Good," I said.

The second picture was of a forest. He said he liked the outdoors and being in the woods.

"Great," I stated.

The next picture was of a hamburger with fries, an advertisement for a national food chain.

"I'm hungry" was all he said, and with that he ripped out the picture and ate it.

"Feel better?" I inquired.

"Not really," he said. "It needed ketchup."

"Clyde," I replied, "I think you can get that and more back at the hospital. Let's go book you a room for a little while longer."

So we did, and Clyde gained the time he needed to get better. Sometimes regressing in life leads to progress.

chapter 96

Erotic or Erratic: What a Difference a Word Makes

W hen I was stationed at Fort Lee, Virginia, as a part of my Army officer training for the Quartermaster Corps, I was assigned to a substance abuse unit. Because we were not always busy, I used to occasionally put on my tennis togs and go play tennis while many of my friends would play golf. Because of this difference in interest, I often went to the courts by myself. My hope was to get involved in a pickup game, and I am pleased to say that frequently happened. However, some times were better than others.

One of my more frustrating experiences came on a windy afternoon in April. I was playing next to another young lieutenant who was quite sincere but not very skilled. She kept hitting her tennis balls over to my court and, of course, kept running over to get them. I would like to report that she finally quit or that she improved, but neither occurred. I can report that she was polite. I tried to be well-mannered in return. However, I finally gave up my game when I realized how futile it was to keep playing under such circumstances.

Well, as fate would have it, a couple of weeks after this incident, I was at a party at the Officers' Club, when who should show up but this same young lieutenant. Seeing me, she waved and came over to where my friends and I were standing. Because she did not have a tennis ball or a tennis racket in her hands, I thought I had nothing to dodge, pick up, or be afraid of.

"I'm really glad to see you," she said. "You left so abruptly the other day. We didn't even have a chance to talk."

"Anyway," she continued, "I just wanted to tell you that I don't think I have ever been as erotic next to anyone in my life as I was with you recently on the tennis court. You were great to keep your sense of humor when I kept messing up. I promise next time I'll be better. I'm practicing."

"Excuse me?" I said.

"I was just too anxious that day," she explained. "If I hadn't been so erotic and broken your concentration, who knows what might have happened."

Well, her sentences kept rolling on, and she kept saying *erotic* for *erratic* until I was blushing pretty badly and my friends were thinking that a love set was more than I had described to them. Finally, I regained my composure and thanked her for her apology. Then I quickly exited her presence once more. However, since that experience I have realized the power of words anew and how different some words that sound similar are from others. I have also been more cognizant that counseling, like life, has its humorous as well as serious moments.

chapter 97

Attitudes

When my oldest son Ben was 16, he came down to breakfast one morning and with a slight growl in his voice said, "Dad, you know the trouble with you? You're too optimistic!"

His words were not meant to be a compliment but I have taken them to be that ever since. "What a wonderful trouble to have," I thought. If the African American spiritual "Nobody Knows De Trouble I've Seen" was referring to people being too optimistic, wouldn't that be better than what trouble usually stands for (i.e., distress, affliction, or danger)?

I believe sometimes it is not what other people say to us but how we receive it that makes a difference in our lives. For instance, if someone were to say that I was clumsy with tools, they would be right. Of course, I could take that as an insult and go hammer them over the head with all my other virtues. I could also decide if someone said this to me that I was going to learn how to use tools more effectively and the result would be that I would sign up for a course in "Tools 101."

The point is that we may become bitter or better as a result of what is conveyed to us through others in our environment. We also do not have to absorb everything that is directed our way or accept it in the way it was meant.

Aaron Beck, Albert Ellis, and cognitive behaviorists as a group have long known what we would be wise to discover and rediscover over time. Attitude goes a long way in directing our mental health and wellness. Optimism, unless wildly overblown, actually seems to have beneficial results. I am glad I have that trouble. I wish everyone did!

chapter 98

The Wearing of Black and Development

*I*n earlier times, people who were in grief over a significant loss, such as that of a family member, wore black as an indicator of their sorrow. Thus, I was surprised when at age 13, my son Tim came down to breakfast wearing a black shirt and slacks. I asked why the outfit, wondering if he was "going Goth." Instead, he replied that Weird Al Yankovich, one of his heroes, had died of carbon monoxide poisoning the night before. After expressing surprise and condolences to Tim, I helped him get ready for the school bus and sent him off.

Afterwards, in looking through the paper, our eldest son Ben, then age 16, discovered that it was one of Weird Al's parents who had died the night before. Apparently, Tim had not heard the radio report just right.

However, then Ben reported what he considered sadder news yet. Victoria's Secret would apparently no longer televise their lingerie show. Although Ben did not go change into black, I could tell he was a bit dismayed.

I guess it all goes to show that what is distressing is different at various ages and stages of development. I am glad Weird Al did not die that day and relieved just a little that Victoria's Secret will no longer display their apparel on a television show my teenage son might watch. Clever songs and "so longs" are always interesting. It is important with both to get the words right, unless you just happen to like to sing your own lyrics or wear the color black like the late Johnny Cash.

chapter 99

Lost

When I lived on the coast of Connecticut, a friend from another region of the country came to visit. He flew into New York and rented a car. However, on his way to my house he got lost.

When the phone rang an hour past the time I expected him, I asked, "John, where are you?"

"I'm at K-Mart," he replied.

Stunned for a minute by his answer, I said, "John, Connecticut is bigger than it looks on the map. We have a lot of K-Marts here. Please give me another landmark so I can help you get to my house."

There was a pause on the line for a few seconds. The next thing I heard was: "Fog-a-re-a. I'm here in Fogarea."

Still confused, I asked him to tell me more about "Fogarea." He then said, "I'm reading a sign. It says 'Fogarea for the next 10 miles.'"

"That's '"fog area,'" I said. "There's a lot of fog here by the water."

Clients sometimes find themselves in similar situations as my friend. They are in new territory. They get lost. One of our responsibilities as counselors is to help them get their bearings and then find direction. It seems so simple in principle, but the process itself is fraught with potential miscues and confusion.

chapter 100

Just Because You're the One and Only Doesn't Mean You Won't Be Left Out Cold and Lonely

A number of years ago, I applied to be the editor of an American Counseling Association (ACA) journal that will remain nameless. It was my second try at becoming a journal editor. Much to my surprise, when the deadline had passed I found that I was the only candidate for the job. Thus, I confidently waited for a letter, a phone call, an e-mail, a visit, or some other personal contact informing me that I (out of default if nothing else) had been appointed editor. An announcement was usually made at the annual convention of the ACA. But instead of receiving a message, the only sound I heard was silence. Furthermore, nothing showed up in my mailbox, at my door, or on my voice mail or computer even though I checked each every few hours.

"Well," I thought. "They must want to wait for a special moment at the convention in order to make the announcement more dramatic."

So, I waited with anticipation of congratulations dancing in my head. However, after awhile, I became frustrated. Finally, I made a call to a person who I knew could tell me what had happened or what was about to occur.

"I'm sorry," was the first phrase I remember that person saying after we had exchanged pleasantries. "You did not get the appointment. We gave it instead to one of our other members who was not a candidate. We just thought it was something we should do even though we would have been fine with you."

The words caught me by surprise but there was virtually nothing I could say in response. I had done all I knew to do and had failed to land the job. It was one of those absurd and unexplainable moments in life.

Since that experience, there have been several other times when I questioned the sanity of humanity and myself because of the illogical and unexplainable nature of events in my universe. To be an "only" is not a guarantee of success. The world does not revolve around logic. As counselors, we should keep that in mind. Many of our clients already know it!

chapter 101

Resiliency and Unpredictability

People are resilient and sometimes solve problems in creative but unpredictable ways. I have found this out with clients and even with members of my own family. Let me illustrate.

Some years ago, my then-preschool second child, Nate, was interested in playing what he described as a "real" game of baseball with me. I tried to dissuade him and just play pitch, but he insisted, even up to the point of calling balls and strikes. Thus, the game began.

I pitched the first ball and Nate swung, missing by a wide margin.

"Strike one," I announced.

I pitched again with the same results.

"Strike two, Nathaniel," I said.

Looking more determined than ever, Nate stepped up to the piece of wood serving as home plate in our front yard. Then I pitched again—a high, slow, floating ball that could have had a sign on it reading "hit me, I'm easy"—but alas, Nate swung and came up empty a third time.

"Strike three," I yelled. "Nate, you are out!"

Nate dropped his bat, hung his head, and slowly started walking away from home plate. I wanted to rescue him and yell, "It's okay. Come back," but I just watched. As I looked on I imagined joining the local chapter of "Bad Parents Anonymous." However, Nate suddenly turned around with a smile on his face, marched confidently back to home plate, picked up the plastic bat he was using, and said, "Dad, I'm a new person."

Sometimes our clients gain a new perspective on an otherwise dismal situation in surprising ways and act accordingly. Being an effective counselor is giving oneself permission to wait for an action as well as to act on a thought, action, or feeling. In such moments, a metamorphosis may occur, and a new person may emerge.

chapter 102

Finding a Vision That Works

It was a minor crisis that, like most crises, started small. I walked quietly into the kitchen one summer morning without making a sound. There was Claire, my wife, looking at a can of tomato soup that she had placed on a counter. Not only was she gazing at the can, but she seemed to be doing a simple dance as well. She would take a step forward every few seconds and then a step back. As opposed to a fox trot, she was doing what I would later describe as a "soup step." However, it was her focus on the soup, not her movement, that caught my attention the most.

"Hmmm," I thought. "Either she likes this tomato soup can and is planning on surprising me with a tangy new breakfast entrée or she is having trouble with her eyes and is trying to find the right spot from which to read the soup's label."

So I asked innocently, "Honey, what are you doing with that can of tomato soup?"

"Nothing," she replied. "I am just checking out the best spot in this kitchen to stand so I can read the soup's contents clearly."

Thus, I knew instantly that any dreams I had of seeing my wife serve a new item on our limited breakfast menu were just that—fantasies. (Cheerios were not disappearing.) Likewise, I breathed a sigh of relief that we would not be going to the Fred Astaire dance studio soon. On the other hand, I knew that the reality of Claire going to see an eye doctor was fairly dim, too. After all, our house had a lot of counters from which cans can be viewed. However, after talking together about the situation, an appointment was made for her to see an optometrist at, of all places, one called VisionWorks. That visit corrected my wife's eye problem, and she began to have even more close encounters with tomato soup cans, packaged foodstuffs, and people.

After a crisis should come a vision, just like after a storm should come a rainbow. If we as counselors are going to be helpful and healing, we need to assist our clients in creating realistic and fulfilling visions and goals. We should encourage them when needed to correct their vision in order to read the fine print as well as to see the big picture. We should do likewise for our own mental health and well-being. Life is good, but to get beyond crises, one needs a focus—a vision, if you will—that goes far beyond kitchen countertops.

Points to Ponder

1. How have you developed personally and professionally in the past few years? Whom do you know who is stuck developmentally, and how do you see yourself and others interacting with that person?

2. What has been your experience in getting lost? How did you feel? What was most helpful to you at such times?

3. Resilience is an important quality in life. When have you seen it displayed in others or yourself? What kind of a difference did it make?

Section | Twelve

LEADERSHIP

If you cannot fly or swim
try walking.

An Old North Carolina Saying

*L*eadership is defined in many ways, but basically leaders envision what a group should be or where it should go. They then provide energy and direction, that is, leadership, in getting those associated with the group's mission to a point or place of action. Leadership is important, in fact crucial, to counselors and the counseling profession. Too often in history, counselors have been passive and have been defined or assigned to situations by others who did not understand what counseling is or what counselors do. The era of passivity is mostly over and now like other professionals in helping, counselors advocate for clients, society at large, and even themselves.

The five vignettes in this section examine leadership from several perspectives, including those related to the personal humanity of the counselor leader. Other topics covered include dealing with the press, being a leader in the midst of or after a crisis, and how leaders may best conceptualize who they are.

chapter 103

The Human Side of Leadership: Being President of the American Counseling Association

$\mathcal{S}$ome people think that being president of the American Counseling Association (ACA) is a one-year term and is mostly cognitive. Actually, it is one term of three years and it has a huge humanistic side, especially if you have a primary relationship and a child or children. Basically, you progress from being president-elect, to president, to past president and you regress to having less time with the ones you love. Each of the segments of this honor has its own challenges and rewards.

To describe what happens in a cryptic way, the duties of the office are somewhat as follows. As president-elect, you get to be an understudy to the president, travel to a number of places, and make a few speeches at various state conferences while standing and being recognized at regional and national conventions. As president, you are the person in charge, get to travel a lot, take initiatives, resolve disputes or disagreements, and make a lot of speeches at regional, state, and national conferences. This year and the president-elect year are the ones that take tons of effort and concentration. They are the ones that require energy, dedication, sacrifice, and a sense of humor. As past president, you get to wish the person who follows you well, travel less, contribute your wisdom when asked, and make a lot of speeches that you could not make as president.

The important point here is realizing that the presidency of the American Counseling Association is both a term and a sentence. It is wonderful and demanding. It is exhilarating and exhausting. It is a one-stop, non-stop, never-slow-down job that is pleasant, profound, and performance-based. It is different from what most people think. Instead of being a king or a queen, you are a prime minister or a secretary of state. Your prime target is promoting counseling, especially ACA. Also, you are a prime target for anyone's discontent, projections, or transference. They know who you are and they know how to reach you. So you are in a position to serve and be served up. That is as inviting and demanding as it ever gets in life.

More experiences happened to me during my time as president than I can possibly describe. You would not get bored reading them or maybe because there are so many of them, you would. I do remember that as president I wanted to emphasize creativity in counseling and made that my theme for the year. Therefore, I had Irvin Yalom give the keynote at the national convention in Atlanta, followed by a panel of creative counselors featuring Jeffrey Kottler, Courtland Lee, Ann Vernon, Daya Sandhu, and Janice Delucia-Waack. I also wanted to produce a public service announcement (PSA) on counseling and thereby enhance ACA's public profile. With the help of Rich Yep, the ACA Executive Director, Melanie Wallace, a counselor volunteer from Alabama, and Chris Knight (a former star of the *Brady Bunch*), we filmed a PSA highlighting the value of counseling in 30-and 60-second spots. It was shown on stations across the United States and was seen in major markets by over 10 million people in its first six months. Had we paid for the air time, it would have cost over $196,000. Instead, the video cost less than $10,000 to produce, was of a high quality, and represented ACA (rather than a person or personality) quite well. Air time was free because it was a PSA.

What else can I say about being ACA president? Well, it had its moments of tension in regard to proposed motions either at the Governing Council or the Council of Presidents and Regional Chairs. Some such motions were aimed at special populations or causes passionately embraced by the presenter. Those were the "sticky" issues. There were also "maverick counselors" who regularly wrote me, usually with outrageous or grandiose ideas, such as giving them money to save part of the planet's population or chastising ACA for not having the same worldview as they had.

Some days I literally came back to my house from the airport, packed or repacked a bag, and was on another plane within hours of landing from the first. Paperwork, e-mails, and phone calls were constant. Delegating was essential. Working with the ACA staff was pleasant and professional. The job was truly a 24/7/365 event and I loved almost every minute of it.

Amid all of the hassle and hurry, there were many touching moments and a number of humorous ones. The most touching came on Christmas Eve when I received an e-mail from a 14-year-old girl whose single-parent mother was drunk and threatening to beat her. Over a couple of hours she was able to pour out her heart. I, in turn, was able to give her some options on what she could realistically do—all over the Internet. In May she wrote me again in regard to how she was following up with Al-Anon and other community service organizations where she lived. Her e-mail then, as now, touched me and I was truly glad I was in the position I was and knew what I did.

On the humorous side, one state conference thoughtfully put a stool behind the podium where I was to speak, believing I would not be able to see over the platform. They were correct. Even though I was hesitant, I climbed the steps and probably gave one of my best keynotes.

Other events in the year flowed together. I kept a journal and recorded thoughts and experiences such as the ones below.

- At a conference in Reno, the first song lyrics I heard in the hotel lobby as I was checking in were "Lord, I was born a gambling man." (If the Allman Brothers could hear themselves now!)
- At another conference in San Francisco the first song I heard was "New York, New York" by Frank Sinatra. (Wrong coast, wrong town, Frank!)
- Once at a convention, I noticed that some numbers on the clock look like groups of people having a discussion, e.g., 503. Others appeared alienated, distant, or isolated from each other, e.g., 984. (Hmm. What did this tell me? Simple. It was time to go home!)
- The longest drive in a rental car I made during the month of November was from Knoxville to Gatlinburg, Tennessee, in a Chevy sub-compact over the mountains and through Dollywood. (I am grateful to still be alive.)
- The longest distance I walked/ran was made at the Maine Counseling Association conference. It was a 5K walk/run. (I'm glad I brought tennis shoes.)
- The most powerful slogan I saw at a conference was "Take your best pony and ride into your worst fear" at the South Dakota Counseling Association Conference.
- The most interesting comments from airlines personnel were: "Don't they ever give you a day off?"—a baggage handler for USAirways.
  "Just leave the lights on and write out a note, we know where you live"—the supervisor for lost luggage at Piedmont Triad Airport.

"It seems like I just saw you yesterday. I did just see you yesterday!"—a TSA screener at the airport.

- The worse flight I experienced: The 7:40 p.m. USAirways flight on September 27, 2004, from Washington, DC, to Greensboro, North Carolina. We tried to land twice in hurricane winds. Then we averted and flew to Norfolk, Virginia. The plane was bouncing up and down and from side to side. People got sick, threw up, screamed, and fainted from the turbulence. We were met on the tarmac by the EMT truck where several people were treated.

- The zones on flights: When an airline told me initially that I was to board by a zone, I expected to look down at my ticket and instead of finding a number, find the word "twilight." As my time as ACA president went on, I found myself upgraded from zone 8 when I began to zone 2, and on occasion, zone 1.

- My favorite movie: *Terminal* with Tom Hanks. (Like Hanks, I learned to live in airports.)

- My favorite night time experiences: Singing karaoke at the New York Counseling Association and at the Maine Counseling Association conferences; dancing at the ACA Convention Opening Party in Atlanta (where I took off my coat and tie while dancing with my wife). I made $4.00 from admiring onlookers who gave me a dollar each as the band sang: "Play that funky music, white boy!"

- My worst dining experience: Eating buffalo at the Carter Center (where I choked and literally had to have the Heimlich maneuver performed on me to get the piece of meat out of my throat).

- My most emotionally moving experiences: Seeing the chair sculptures at night at the Oklahoma City National Memorial and touring the museum the next day; seeing the World War II Memorial in DC at night

- The best game my three children played when I was on ACA trips: Where in the world is Dad tonight? (The first guess was usually "Washington, DC.") They played this game putting a wooden snowman in my chair at the dinner table.

- My worst experience returning home (besides lost luggage): Having our sheltie bark at me as if I were a stranger. She managed to wake everyone up in the process.

Altogether I made a total of 93 ACA-related trips during my tenure with 266 legs/links/connecting flights. My theme song was Willie Nelson's "On the Road Again." I always took with me my computer, a cell phone, my presentation(s) on a flash drive, overheads, written remarks, comments, and speeches. I stayed in both beautiful and less than spectacular rooms. I once stayed in a honeymoon suite in Coeur d'Alene, Idaho. It was spectacular (especially the mirror on the ceiling), but I am afraid it was a waste since I was by myself and in the 20th year of my marriage. Regardless, being the ACA president not only taught me a lot about counseling, it also taught me a lot about being human!

chapter 104

Dealing With the Press Can Be a Mess— But You Should Do It

Being on television or in the newspaper can seem like a dream. However, it can sometimes be a nightmare. I have had "good press days" and "God help me press days." Two of the latter are chronicled here—one being with the visual press (that is, television) and the other with the printed press (that is, newspapers).

In television it is customary to come into a studio, be greeted, be introduced to the interviewer, respond, and leave. It seems so simple on the surface. But what appears to be is not always what is. For example, after working in a disaster mental health area, I was contacted and asked to talk about the experience on the early evening news of the primary station in my city. I was a little hesitant initially but acquiesced. Fifteen minutes before the appointed time of the interview, I was just completing a guest appearance in another professor's classroom, so I really had to hustle to get to the television studio on time. Fortunately, I made it with a couple of minutes to spare. I was greeted and escorted back to a room near the main studio. There I was told I had a couple of minutes before I was to be on air. As I tried to get my thoughts together I realized I was doing so amid the buzz and blaring sound of three televisions sets tuned into the early evening news show. Thus, I struggled to focus. To make matters worse, the two minutes were boiled down to one.

So, I went to meet the co-anchors, sat in my chair, and buttoned my coat, and then came two surprises. The first was that the director noticed I was not sitting on the same level with the anchors. (I was not blessed with any kind of rear end.) So, he quickly improvised and to elevate me, he brought in a copy of *The Real Yellow Pages* (I am glad they were not *The Phony Yellow Pages*). Quietly but firmly he said, "Sit on it," which I did (as if responding to The Fonz on the television show *Happy Days*).

Then one of the co-anchors leaned over and said, "Have you seen the questions we are going to ask?"

"No," I responded only to hear the producer start counting backwards:

"10-9-8-7...."

Well, to say the interview was less than an Emmy Award–winning experience would be an understatement. It lasted about two minutes but seemed like two hours. I can only imagine that the ratings for the show plummeted with every syllable I spoke. I am glad to report, however, that I did not slip off my phonebook, as I hung on to it and the few coherent thoughts I could muster from queries that must have been formulated at 4:00 in the morning by an apprentice. When asked later how the experience went, I simply replied that I felt like it had been an "uplifting and gripping event."

That response was quite the opposite of one I had with the national press or should I say a prominent-for-its-time tabloid that focused more on sensationalism than facts. Yes, against my better judgment I did an interview with a reporter for this "check-out-at-the-supermarket-next-to-the-candy-and-glamour magazines rag." A few weeks later, nestled next to a story entitled "Aliens Dressed Like Alligators Taking Over Alaska," was the feature story for which I was partially responsible for generating. It was on relationships.

As far as I know, the narrative was read and received well by all but one person, a woman from Pennsylvania. She thought it was trash and wrote the president of my university stating so. Her letter might have been thrown away or quickly discarded except for one small fact. I was his assistant and occupied the office next to him. So when he came waltzing through my open door waving a letter and asking me about what I had said, I found myself at a loss for words. If the ground could have swallowed me up, I would have gone under gratefully. However, that did not happen and it took me a long time to respond. I finally replied, "I have not seen the story. What angle did the reporter take? I don't know the woman who has complained."

Then my boss explained and expounded on what had been written by the newspaper and the woman. The paper had apparently interpreted the meaning of my thoughts liberally, and the woman who had responded saw no parallels in the affection chickens show for each other and what adults display toward one another.

Then it struck me. I had been talking about children, but the paper had printed the word *chicken*. The fact that no one else had picked up on this mistake (or at least written the president of my university) still baffles me. I was raised in the city. I know nothing about chickens. However, I am the father of three children and I think I do know a little something about *them*.

So, my advice on responding to a request for an interview related to counseling (or anything counseling related) is "Do it, but be cautious!"

Ask to see a copy of questions beforehand if possible and a rough draft of what will be printed before the presses roll. Never pass up a chance to clarify what you said. Otherwise you may end up in a stew with a superior asking you to explain the unexplainable while you vow silently to yourself never to go to Pennsylvania, eat chicken, or use *The Real Yellow Pages* again!

chapter 105

The Leader as a Catalyst and Servant

*Leadership is the act of working in such a way
that people and possibilities are brought together
in a positive and productive manner.*

Quickly now, name the 33rd president of the American Counseling Association! How about the 33rd president of the United States? Okay, how about the 11th president of either entity? Give up? I don't blame you. Fame is fleeting. Most of us do not "chunk" into our long-term memories the names of leaders unless they have been heroic, such as Abraham Lincoln, or they left their office in disgrace, like Richard Nixon. The reason is fairly simple. We have too many other people and events to remember that are more relevant to our lives. Thus, individual names on the tip of our tongues for a moment usually, over time, become lost in the recesses of our minds.

Therefore, leaders and aspiring leaders take note. Despite the lyrics of the song "Fame," the majority of us do not "live forever" in the collective memories of most people. That being the case, *Why lead?*

Just like the motivations to become a counselor, some reasons for aspiring to leadership are healthier than others. Among the best are wanting to make a positive (and hopefully lasting) contribution to the entity of which you are a part. When such is the motivation to lead, the result is often a loss of self within the group. The person becomes immersed in the process of making the group better without becoming concerned for individual recognition. Thus, there is a "flow," where the person and the entity come together in a synergistic way. In such a process the leader is a catalyst and a servant. He or she brings people, resources, and ideas together with little concern for fanfare or flaunting. Yet, the investment in the purpose and causes of the group bring the leader great inner joy and contentment while furthering the cause of those being served. Who are people like that? How about Dag Hammerskjold, the former Secretary General of the United Nations; Mother Teresa, truly a "saint" to the poorest of the poor in Calcutta; Martin

Luther King Jr., the leading civil rights leader of the 20th century; Sequoyah, the creator of the Cherokee alphabet; Cesar Chavez, an indefatigable organizer of migrant Chicano farm workers in California; or Gilbert Wrenn and Mary Thomas Burke, who were tireless, warm, and insightful advocates for counseling.

While these individuals had personal flaws, all were focused on goals outside of themselves. They were aware, in the lyrics of Neil Diamond, that life is "done too soon," and delaying what can be undertaken now may mean never accomplishing anything. They may also have read the writings of Abraham Maslow or Robert Greenleaf, both of whom asserted that a meaningful existence focuses on "we" and not "me." Such a stance concentrates on causes full of caring and concern for the betterment of all people. As counselors, we can become such catalysts and servant leaders. The question is "How?"

There is no simple answer to the how question but as in counseling, there are a number of valid approaches. One way is for leaders to show through their behaviors what needs to be done (i.e., leadership by example). This approach can stand alone or even more effectively be combined with leaders "telling and selling" (i.e., explaining and motivating) others to imagine and work toward a vision. Therefore, an excellent strategy on how to lead is for leaders to always do first what they ask of followers while helping members understand the rationale behind the actions. In that way everyone becomes mentally, emotionally, and behaviorally engaged. For example, if the task is for members of an association to lobby for passage of a bill in a legislative session, ideally the leader is at the forefront of the delegation explaining why the group is assembled and the importance of the task ahead. Then the leader energetically moves with the group to the offices of legislators who need to be contacted and makes needed points with the legislator during the visit while urging others to speak as well.

Staying on task and on target is another undertaking leaders need to carry out. While world peace is a noble cause, most groups do not have the resources to be successful in undertaking this agenda effectively. Similarly, while it may be fun to entertain oneself or guests when in a leadership role, that is not the purpose of being in the position. Thus, keeping on course is crucial to the success of leaders and their groups. Within the American Counseling Association (ACA), the mission is to "enhance the quality of life in society by promoting the development of professional counselors, advancing the counseling profession, and using the profession and practice of counseling to promote respect for human dignity and diversity." That is a worthy goal!

Finally, leaders need to have the diplomacy and tact to bring members of a common cause along developmentally and socially so that they, the leaders, are not alone in their striving. That ability is easier to conceptualize than to implement. It takes constant monitoring and a lot of input and energy. The building of relationships occurs gradually. However, as counselors we have learned relationship and empathy skills. If we utilize these processes, we will be able to gauge where members of our groups are and hopefully respond constructively. Whether at a branch, division, national, or even international level, leadership is manifested much better and more strongly if rapport and empathy are a part of the foundation on which it is built.

The right kind and style of leadership can go far in generating or perpetuating an association and its agenda. ACA is an association that is healthy and growing but it is in constant need of new, dynamic, and selfless leaders. We need volunteers who will lead in an altruistic fashion. My belief is that potential leaders would do well first to examine their motives. While few of us are "pure" and none of us are "flawless," striving to be a leader means yearning to take care of business and others before attending to any individual needs besides those that keep a person healthy. Leadership often entails being a catalyst and a servant. While leading is not without its rewards, it strikes me that the satisfaction is best if it is internalized in the heart of the leader and not worn on one's sleeve. After all, who was the 33rd president of the ACA or even the USA?

Note: From Gladding, S. T. (2004c, October). The leader as a catalyst and servant. *Counseling Today*, p. 5.

chapter 106

Leadership in Counseling After a Crisis

She stands
leaning on his outstretched arm
sobbing awkwardly
Almost suspended between
the air and his shoulder
like a leaf being blown
in the wind from a branch
at the end of summer.
He tries to give her comfort
quietly offering up soft words
and patting her head arrythmically.
"It's okay," he whispers
realizing that as the words leave his mouth
he is lying
And that their life together has collapsed
like the South Tower of the World Trade Center
that killed their only son.

*L*iterally thousands of words have been written about the tragedy of the September 11th terrorists' attack on the World Trade Center, Hurricane Katrina, and the April 2007 shootings at Virginia Tech. The incidents stunned us and still seem incomprehensible. We watched much of what happened on television yet even now we still have a hard time believing our eyes even when we see replays. The magnitude of the events and the sheer number of people killed and injured were so great as to seem, at first glance, fictitious. However, with each passing day, news accounts revealed to us in graphic and personal details the realities of these incidents. All of us are still involved as participants in some way as we continue to witness them and relive in our minds the horror of each that left us in shock, sorrow, and sadness. The world changed and became more unsafe and unstable in these senseless sacrifices of innocent people.

In response to what we witnessed and felt, many of us did something constructive. We were able to in a number of ways. We joined together in making donations to the families of the victims, giving blood to support the hospitals and Red Cross workers who were attending the wounded, and writing letters to support the rescue workers as well as to console those who had lost loved ones. There were teach-ins that we participated in, too. These activities were therapeutic both for us as givers and for those who were the recipients of our efforts.

Another chance to serve came in the leadership area as some of us were able to volunteer in the hardest hit areas. I was not able to work with victims of Hurricane Katrina, but when I was asked to go to New York to work as a mental health technician for the American Red Cross and later to work as a disaster mental health worker at Virginia Tech, I did not hesitate. These were opportunities that I realized would not come again. They were important to answer positively. So, I got my credentials together quickly and made arrangements.

In New York, I started on the 15th day after the attack. That day the emphasis of the search at the World Trade Centers went from rescue to recovery. My assigned site was in the Family Assistance Center on Pier 94, where families of victims went to apply for death certificates. There I saw survivors of the tragedy and worked with them to help process the wide range of feelings—from denial to grief—that they felt. My initial job was to assist individuals make applications for death certificates of their loved ones. In that capacity I was an escort who walked with families from the front of the building to the back and talked with them about what they were feeling, what they had felt, or what they anticipated doing in regard to the emotions that would be coming. I also accompanied families to Ground Zero so they could see for themselves the horror and finality of the event. The view of the site helped many individuals begin the process of grieving in depth as they realized, in a stark and striking way, that those they had loved and cherished in so many ways were indeed dead and would not be coming back to be with them.

At Virginia Tech, I worked with others in helping students, staff, and faculty resume classes and their lives a week after the shootings. I talked with individuals on the parade field who seemed lost or in a state of grief. I went into classrooms, with the permission of professors, and spoke with students about classmates they had lost and what they could do now in the wake of a wave of sorrow. Sometimes, I just stood and let people approach me because I was identified, like others, with a purple armband. Unlike New York, the Virginia Tech experience was more cut up into blocks of time—the two days when classes resumed, graduation, and then pro bono counseling for survivors of the aftermath that summer.

From these experiences and other related incidents, I learned a great deal more than I ever anticipated about the nature of counseling, clients, and even myself. In what follows, I will describe what I became most aware of during this time and immediately following. These lessons have some universal application for persons who enter almost any crisis situation. They are especially applicable to crises that may seem on the surface overwhelming.

The first lesson I gleaned from my time as a grief and crisis counselor is the realization of how crucial the personhood of the counselor is. I knew this fact going in but I relearned it time and time again. There are many people who have technical skills that are helpful in times of need. However, in dealing with individuals who are traumatized, the first critical factor that comes to the forefront is the mental health of the person who would be a helper. A counselor who has difficulty dealing with the rawness of feelings or who is put off with severe emotional pain is unable to function adequately, let alone effectively, in such circumstances. Therefore, it is crucial that in a crisis situation a counselor be ready physically, mentally, and behaviorally. Health within the person of the counselor fosters the ability to reach out in a way that facilitates growth for those in need.

Besides the integrative and healthy nature of the counselor as a person, another essential element of the process of helping in the midst of crisis and pain is in the interpersonal domain. A counselor who tries to do everything ends up not doing anything worthwhile in the short run and becomes a burden to others. Therefore, those who choose to work in crises must quickly build a sense of support through interpersonal relationships with other professionals. The good news is that such alliances are often easier to forge in these times because of the cooperative spirit among professionals that transcends turf wars and any pettiness that might otherwise be present. That was the case in New York, Virginia Tech, and, from what my colleagues tell me, in the aftermath of Hurricane Katrina.

Another response to a crisis, I realized anew, is that of flexibility. The circumstances under which clients arrive for assistance in times such as these are not ideal. People arrive in many states of mind. Some are in denial. Some are angry. Others are alone or psychologically separate. To assist them in expressing their grief, we who are mental health workers must show leadership by staying fluid in regard to what we do. As professionals we have to be ready to deal with anything. Being ready to appropriately respond to the novel and unexpected is a necessary requirement for this work, and is forced to the forefront of needed skills.

Knowing follow-up resources and persons is a similar needed skill that I realized anew from my work at these sites of tragedy. I was from out-of-state, and therefore it was necessary for me to link those I worked with to practitioners and mental health facilities in their own neighborhoods so they would have support after I left and not flounder around without adequate resources. As professionals, we know we need links to community agencies and specialists. We gather that data over time and usually gradually. In crisis counseling, the speed at which this task must be completed is greatly accelerated as is its significance.

The importance of small acts of kindness is another point I repeatedly noted in the aftermath of the tragedy sites where I worked. People were appreciative of such gestures in ways that were unexpected. For example, handing clients individually wrapped packages of tissues inevitably brought remarks of gratitude from clients with whom I worked. Words of condolence, such as "I am sorry for your loss," seemed deeply appreciated. It may well be that the brutality that had beaten these people down made them more open and receptive to these simple actions. Regardless, these uncomplicated acts of kindness seem to be beneficial in not only establishing rapport but also starting the healing process.

Nonverbals were essential, too. Some of these acts, but by all means not all of them, were received in a different way than anything I have witnessed before. These types of communication took the usual forms, such as a touch on the shoulder, support of an arm, or a simple glance conveying empathy. In New York, they also took the shape of giving small stuffed bears or Beanie Babies to children and their parents as we walked past reminders of those who had died, such as walls with pictures of the missing on them. At Virginia Tech, they were more in the form of writing remembrances at makeshift memorials or lending a student or faculty your undivided attention as they talked. Regardless, recipients seemed to be deeply touched, possibly because of what they were experiencing in regard to sight, sound, and touch. The nonverbal signals seemed to be picked up gratefully as well as quickly.

The final lesson that comes to mind in regard to my times at these places is that of being especially mindful of taking care of myself as a person and a professional. In crisis there is a tendency to sometimes try to display "the hero syndrome," where one does without needed essentials such as nourishment and sleep. While such behavior may yield something in the short run, it is devastating in the long run because the hero ends up burning out, blowing up, or bowing out because of a lack of stamina. There were only a very few people I saw who tried to be heroes like this, although the temptation was tantalizingly available. Instead of yielding to such temptation, I and others found that walking to and from work, writing in a journal regularly, taking needed nourishment, and debriefing with professionals on site enabled us to maintain a positive outlook, maintain our health, and deal with the affect and behavior that constantly came before us.

Overall, in the midst of working with people who are in a crisis, there are a number of important things to keep in mind. Some of these are obvious. Others are surprising. All are essential. It is critical that in a 9/11, Hurricane Katrina, or Virginia Tech–type incident that counselors make sure they

- are mentally healthy to begin with,
- interact in positive and professional ways with colleagues,
- stay flexible and be ready for the unexpected,
- learn resources and people within the community to whom they can make referrals,
- realize the power and potential of small acts of kindness, such as a sympathetic word,
- are mindful of the influence of nonverbal actions that lend support to those in need, from giving them tissues to offering them symbols of comfort such as stuffed bears, and
- take care of themselves through physical exercise, keeping a journal, taking in needed nourishment, and debriefing regularly.

In summary, counseling after a crisis is a time filled with heavy emotion. It is a time of opportunity as well as turmoil. It demands much of us who are counselors. Knowing what to expect can make the experience more productive and not being afraid to show leadership in working with others in pain can make such time transformational.

Note. Adapted from Gladding, S. T. (2002). Reflections on counseling after the crisis. In G. R. Walz & C. J. Kirkman (Eds.), *Helping people cope with tragedy and grief* (pp. 9–12). Greensboro, NC: CAPS.

chapter 107

Smoke and Mirrors

Sometimes my colleagues tease me about "neither slumbering nor sleeping" at night since I have tended to be very productive on a number of fronts. In the bantering that has gone on about how I can do so much, I have occasionally responded flippantly. On one such occasion I told the department's program manager that I did everything with "smoke and mirrors." She laughed. Later, when someone asked her about how I managed to be so productive, she jokingly repeated the phrase.

Probably nothing would have happened after that except as in the game "rumor," the phrase "smoke and mirrors" got twisted around. Thus, at a national event, I had a good friend come up to me with a distressed look on his face and a deep concern in his voice.

"I heard how you've been getting your work done," he said. "I hear you've been smoking marijuana!"

Well, I could have died but I thought better of it. Later my friend felt like dying but could not and did not. When he heard what phrase I had originally said in jest, he just gave out a big sigh, threw up his hands, and walked away shaking his head from side to side and mumbling, "I should never have believed that story. I got smoked!"

On my part, maybe I should never have uttered the phrase "smoke and mirrors." It seemed light-hearted but it turned out to result in a heavy heart for my friend. Since that incident, I have renewed my effort not to believe everything I hear. Like smoke, some accounts of action are cloudy and full of hot air. Like mirrors, some descriptions of events only reflect part of the truth. The rest is hidden and only discovered through direct interactions. Whether with colleagues or clients, we are wise to not assume or to be presumptuous. Sometimes things "just are" and cannot be explained away or described beyond the facts.

Points to Ponder

1. What do you know about the personal side of leaders? How do you think occurrences outside of the spotlight of being a leader affect those who are leaders? What roles do you suppose family and friends play in the effectiveness of leaders?

2. What do you think about the media and the way it presents news? What sources do you think portray news stories most fairly and accurately? What might you do if an interview you gave was distorted?

3. Sometimes leaders call attention to themselves and highlight their accomplishments. What do you think of leaders who engage in this type of activity? What leaders do you know, in any field, who have focused on being catalysts or servants to their constituents?

ISSUES IN COUNSELING

All those Virginians who now live with me
through history and memory
have come to life collectively
as I walk the streets of Alexandria.
Complementary and estranged
their surnames flow and rearrange my thoughts
to focus on who they were in their time
and who they hoped or wished to be.

—Gladding, © 2008[11]

ounseling is multidimensional. It has many branches and it is likewise of interest to numerous constituencies. Counseling incorporates social justice, multiculturalism, mental health, and career developmental dimensions under its broad umbrella. More importantly, counseling, or counselling as it is spelled in countries outside the United States, is international. It is a positive and productive force for the good of many societies.

The vignettes in this section examine counseling both internally and externally. All too often, counselors have been divided in their efforts to bring about change for the good of others. Frequently, egos have gotten in the way of transformative changes. Yet despite their shortcomings, counseling and counselors have made a difference in many domains. This "quiet revolution" is one that will continue to be a powerful force.

chapter 108

Counseling as a Quiet Revolution

He tries to explain the pain
but like attempting to describe gray skies and rain
his words fall short of their goal
and hit the ground with an empty sound.
She listens, reflects, and helps direct
the session beyond raw hurt.
Together they move toward solution;
counseling is a quiet revolution.

When most of us hear the word "revolution," we do not think of counseling. The reason is that our mental association with the "R" word is primarily tied to orbital motions or the overthrow of governments. Thus, we talk about the revolving of planets and historical uprisings in the establishments of nations such as France or the United States. Yet, counseling at its best is revolutionary. It is a discovery process that ultimately changes people by disrupting the axis around which they revolve, such as obsession, depression, and anxiety. The disruption results in an uprising against the restraints that have held them back, for instance, negative thoughts or hostile environments. Hence, counseling involves the rotating in a person's life of cognitions, emotions, and behaviors, as well as the ouster of self-defeating habits, irrational mandates, and environmental restraints. In a word, counseling is "radical!"

Yet, the process of counseling is seldom noisy—at least as perceived by the public. That is because it usually takes place in calm surroundings, such as the privacy of an office. Consequently, counseling can be conceptualized as a quiet helping profession with a profound impact. It is experienced directly by those involved in it and indirectly by those who are recipients of its impact. The result is that counseling is felt throughout the environments in which it is conducted. Everyone benefits.

So how does it happen? Well, sometimes it happens through trial and error. Usually, however, theories and relationships are at the heart of the process of change, as are universal helping skills. The experience of the counselor and the readiness of clients play a part, too.

If counseling is constructive, clients grow and open up. They make purposeful decisions. They stop behavior that is destructive and non-productive, such as fighting, being passive, or just blabbering. They quit trying to externally control others and begin taking charge of themselves. They assess and utilize their strengths. Outside of sessions, they practice new behaviors through role plays and simulations. They confront injustices and abuse. They give themselves permission to seek wellness. The outcome is substantial, for old habits become history and new skills, realities, and lifestyles emerge.

I experienced the quiet transformational power of counseling a number of years ago when I met a middle-aged woman at a social. She knew me and asked if I remembered her. I was clueless. Therefore, she reintroduced herself through a story. Years before she was a living wreck with bad breath, greasy hair, and appalling behavior. People avoided her because she was likely to say or do anything that was unpleasant, inappropriate, or ugly. They called her names that ended in the letters "itch." However, as the pain of rejection and discomfort grew, she sought out the services of a counselor. Her therapy helped her modify her actions and looks. Her self-concept rose. Her health improved. She established a new circle of friends and created a productive life.

Granted, most shifts in life are not as remarkable or dramatic. However, even small adjustments can make a huge difference. For instance, learning to reflect instead of bursting out in anger or overreacting in a hostile way can change the tone and tenor of any relationship. So even though our services may not make the front page of the *New York Times* or be the lead story on the NBC Nightly News, what we do in counseling is innovative, inspirational, and important. We help people alter their lives for the better. We assist individuals in envisioning who they can be. We pave the way for possibilities. We confront injustices in society and help overthrow them. We support persons throughout their lives in finding wellness.

These types of changes are rewarding. They are the start of positive individual, group, family, and environment modifications. So, from pain that is often internally ingrained, client growth emerges. The outcome is usually quiet, often revolutionary, but most significantly, life changing!

Note. From Gladding, S. T. (2005d, May). Counseling as a quiet resolution. *Counseling Today,* p. 5.

chapter 109

Counseling in an Age of Chaos: Learning From a Historical Perspective

*W*e live in a time of duress with many people displaying primary and secondary symptoms of posttraumatic stress. We are surrounded by media that pick up and sometimes amplify the uncertainties of life and the tragic nature of human folly. In print, in pictures, in voice, and in video, we experience firsthand what damage ignorance, intolerance, revenge, and hatred can do. Not surprisingly, many among us become stressed with the unrest that has become a part of our daily existence.

So, what can counseling and counselors say to the news of the day? What can we bring to the bitterness that divides persons on both domestic and international fronts? How do we personally and professionally cope and even grow when there is so much that is counterproductive to our survival and development? It seems to me that part of the answer is found within our own history and the examples of men and women who did the best of things in the worst of times.

When we examine the roots of our profession, they are based initially on the work of three individuals who lived with vision and purpose. This trinity of pioneers was composed of Frank Parsons, Clifford Beers, and Jesse B. Davis. Individually they accomplished much; collectively they left a legacy for us to celebrate and enrich. They all made their most distinguishing contributions around the time that Howard Taft was elected and sworn in as President of the United States (1908–1909). So what did they do? Outwardly their deeds were notable, but it is the ideas that they left behind that have the most implications for us today regardless of our age, stage in life, or cultural background.

After going through a number of jobs—civil engineer, school teacher, attorney, and college professor—Frank Parsons settled down, and through his work with young people, he constructed a theory of career development. His involvement in the Boston Vocational Bureau and the publication of his book, *Choosing a Vocation*, were two important events in his life. However, as important as Parsons's theory of careers was and is, I think Parsons might best be remembered for his emphasis on having choices in life. If we wish, we may cower and resign ourselves to fate.

An approach of this type might be justified given the world in which we live. However, Parsons not only highlighted the importance of choice, but also called attention to the significance of meaningfulness in life. It was Parsons who stressed that it is better to find something to do that is meaningful than to entrust your life to the whims of chance and the will of others.

Clifford Beers was likewise someone who rose up against the norms of the status quo and did something significant. Hospitalized for mental illness, specifically depression and paranoia, Beers observed the horrors of institutionalization firsthand. He saw some mental patients having to sleep in straitjackets, tightened to the point of inhibiting the circulation in their hands. He observed others being locked for days in an unheated room, clothed only in their underwear. He witnessed the beating of disobedient patients who were so far out of their minds they could not comprehend or obey orders. Through his struggles, suffering, and misery, Beers was able to shed light on a process that treated people as less than human. His revelations and recommendations appealed to the conscience of America, and major reforms were initiated. He started the Connecticut Society for Mental Hygiene, the National Committee for Mental Hygiene (now, the National Mental Health Association), and the International Congress for Mental Hygiene. His emphasis on promoting mental health and his humanitarian spirit still influence counseling today.

Finally, there is Jesse B. Davis. Unlike Parsons and Beers, Davis lived a more conventional life. He was a class counselor at Central High School in Detroit, Michigan, from 1898 to 1907. In this role, he was responsible for educational and vocational counseling with 11th-grade boys and girls. In 1907, however, he became the principal of a high school in Grand Rapids, Michigan. In this role, Davis began a school-wide guidance program where English teachers included guidance lessons in their composition classes to help students develop character, avoid problem behaviors, and relate vocational interests to curriculum subjects. Thus, Davis highlighted prevention and preparation for life. He can be characterized as a promoter of prosocial and proactive programs that developmentally included children. Interestingly and importantly, Davis offered services, as did Parsons and Beers, to people from all backgrounds.

So what lessons can we take from these individuals of yesterday? After all, they made their impact on our profession over 100 years ago! It was a time before there was an Office of Homeland Security and a great fear of terrorism.

First, even though they lived before our time of great change and uncertainty, each early founder of our profession had a vision of what could be. None of them accepted reality as it was. They saw deplorable conditions but they did not succumb to them. They witnessed inhumane actions but they did not participate in them. They talked to people who were adrift but they did not lose their sense of purpose. Instead, they forged new paths. They set out to establish new ways of working with people. They saw the possible. Therefore, Parsons envisioned a way of making career decisions, Beers visualized a novel approach to working with people with mental disorders, and Davis perceived a fresh means by which to prepare young people to live responsible lives.

A second parallel we see in these people is that of a positive emphasis. Each of these persons could have whined and complained. They were up against overwhelming odds. They had few assets outside of themselves. Yet, they marshaled their internal and external resources to the greatest extent possible. With passion and compassion they stressed meaningfulness, choice, positive mental health, humane interaction, growth, prevention, and the acquiring of skills for living. Thus, we find an emphasis not just on surviving but on living productively. Parsons was the most restless, Beers was the most tormented, and Davis the most tranquil. However, each of these persons saw life as a productive process. They reflected and after gathering their thoughts, they acted purposefully.

Third, these pioneers either established or worked through a system. Parsons worked through the Boston Vocational Bureau, Beers established mental health associations, and Davis created an outlet for his ideas through the public schools. The important thing is that none of these people tried to do things alone. The result is that their efforts have lasted and inspired others.

Fourth, all were advocates. They believed deeply in what they were doing and how they were accomplishing their goals. Parsons and Beers wrote books; Davis spread the word of what he believed through the system in which he found himself. We should do no less.

Finally, a lesson we see in each of these individuals is that in uncertain times, creativity and persistence are called for, and when called forth, both have a calming effect on the populace. For instance, Frank Parsons was constantly recreating himself and in so doing helped others create themselves calmly. Likewise, Clifford Beers was creative in warning others how they might lose their lives and humanity if they did not join with him in forming associations to combat the degrading of persons who were helpless and in hopeless surroundings. Jesse B. Davis was similar to his contemporaries in formulating a time, place, and space for growth and working with people already in place (i.e., teachers) to accomplish his vision.

In conclusion, I think there are several points that we can draw from briefly examining the lives of those who founded our profession. Like us, our predecessors lived in troubled and turbulent times. Their era was filled with massive immigration, industrialization, and movement/migration from farms to cities. There was considerable unrest and abuse in their day. However, these individuals focused on what they could do rather than on their fears, frustrations, or failures.

Regardless of who we are, if we are to become effective, we would do well to claim Counseling and Counselor as our professional names and stake out our lineage in the tradition of Parsons, Beers, and Davis. We have a historical heritage of which we can be proud and one that points us towards a greater good regardless of our circumstances or present conditions.

Note. From Gladding, S. T. (2005a, January). Counseling in an age of chaos. *Counseling Today*, p. 5.

chapter 110

Counseling in Context: Keeping a Balance

ounseling is described in a number of ways. It is portrayed as a helping profession that is diverse and wide-ranging in regard to topics covered and populations served. It is seen as consisting primarily of theories and techniques for treating individuals, groups, and families in stress. For some, the profession is action-oriented with an emphasis on promoting social justice and making strategic interventions in society. Still others highlight counseling within narrower bands in specific settings, such as educational institutions, health clinics, or hospitals. For a fifth group, counseling is a profession that focuses on development, wellness, and prevention—with wholeness as a primary emphasis. Yet a final cluster sees counseling as an outcome research discipline related to the changes people make as a result of investigated and statistically proven therapeutic interventions. Therefore, when anyone asks what counseling is, the response is often a definition that is partially true but not entirely accurate or comprehensive. In fact, counseling encompasses all of the processes, interventions, and focal points just mentioned. It is more than the sum of its parts.

A common factor in counseling, regardless of how it is conceptualized, is the emphasis within the profession on helping people to engender or discover meaning in their lives. People live better and society benefits from such lives when individuals have a purpose that goes beyond themselves and their immediate needs. That thread is one in the fabric of counseling that has extended long and strong through the profession's history. For instance, we find luminaries, such as Gilbert and Kathleen Wrenn, among others, emphasizing repeatedly the need for individuals to formulate and follow a higher purpose for life, to give to others, and to invest their time productively.

With its emphasis on meaningfulness, the profession of counseling can be seen as a movement toward overthrowing superficial values, ranging from acquiring greater wealth to whiter teeth. The goal is to replace these lightweight obsessions with a deeper emphasis that involves the discovery of what a person can do to make a difference in the world. Therefore, in working with clients, ourselves, and our profession comprehensively, we need to see not only the turmoil without but also within. When such is the case, we can be more empathic and thus help chart new directions.

People move on when their pain has been transformed from self-centered hurt to hope and renewal. The movement and change that goes on in individuals is often subtle like a mild breeze on a summer morning. Like such a wind, the change that results is refreshing. However, it may be so understated that it almost goes unnoticed. My two oldest children illustrated that to me when they were toddlers and I was trying to get them to bed. Ben, my oldest and at the time age 3, said, "Daddy, it is white dark. Soon it will be blue dark. We go to bed at black dark."

He was right. The light at dusk changes slowly but significantly, somewhat like people with whom we work and much like ourselves and, at times, the world.

There will always be man-made and natural events, from those that are enlightening to those that are frightening. New plays, paintings, and music will entertain us. Terrorism and the tragedy of school shootings will upset and tear us apart. Random and senseless acts of violence are something we cannot control directly but they are events that we can constructively address. The physical and emotional needs of people around the world call for our help in many ways. In varied communities, we can offer immediate relief and long-term support.

Counseling provides mending and meaningfulness in a broken and a directionless world. Regardless of its context, counseling is a valued commodity.

chapter 111

Diagnosis, Labels, and Dialogue

She was lonely so she cut herself
to get her friends' attention,
He was scared so he hit someone
and now he has detention,
Neither one knew what to do
so they did their best,
The trouble is now they wear labels:
"Different from the rest!"

When I began my career in counseling, I was quickly introduced to the *Diagnostic and Statistical Manual of Mental Disorders* (*DSM*), which continues to come out in new editions and revisions.

"This is the holy book of all helping professionals," my director noted. "It would be good if you memorized it but if you don't, won't, or can't I suggest you keep it on your desk and refer to it often. All the animals aren't in the zoo."

I did not memorize the *DSM* then nor do I plan to now. It is, as my supervisor implied, "an important book." It is likewise a controversial book because of the categories it includes and excludes and the nomenclature of its many diagnoses. In all fairness, we as helping professionals need ways to classify people with whom we work. Otherwise, our efficiency and effectiveness may be impaired. Diagnosing is an essential part of counseling.

The question is whether the *DSM* is the most appropriate way to consistently do that. The subject continues to be the topic of spirited debates. I will not focus on the *DSM* here as much as I will focus on diagnoses and labels and the way they impact counseling for better and worse.

My first adventure into diagnosis was when I was 16 and saw the movie *West Side Story*. It moved me in more ways than any movie or play since because of its emphasis on love, hate, culture, caring, and social justice. One of the more clever songs in the film was "Officer Krupke." The lyrics centered around the maladies of a gang member in New York. The problem was that he was diagnosed differently by each "professional" who evaluated him with the crescendo of the number summing up the results as

> "The trouble is he's lazy
> The trouble is he drinks
> The trouble is he's crazy
> The trouble is he stinks...."

Obviously, there were a number of ways to diagnosis or define this young man. Was one more correct than the others? Were dual or multiple diagnoses most appropriate? Moreover, were the diagnoses helpful?

Again, in some cases the *DSM* is essential in what we do and how we accomplish our goals. It is difficult, if not impossible, to formulate a treatment plan if we are not sure what we are treating. On the other hand, a diagnosis can get in the way of promoting health and wellness.

Labels are also filled with potential and pitfalls. Growing up, I remember some of the more popular labels to which I was exposed. For example, a television commercial insisted that if a canned product had "Libby's on the label" I would "love what was on the table." Likewise, a local department store claimed that if a box said "Rich's on the outside," I would "love what's on the inside."

The trouble with these labels and many others is that they are simplistic and often wrong. I neither loved Libby's beets nor the clothes I would discover in Rich's boxes when I was young. The fact is that people are more complex than the words we use to describe them.

Furthermore, the labels we employ may be both degrading and inappropriate. For instance, if we can call our enemies names such as "gooks," we dehumanize them to the point where we lessen our guilt in fighting or even killing them. Likewise, labeling another counselor as "crazy," or categorizing them in other derogatory terms if they disagree with us is to pigeonhole someone and justify attacks that may or may not be constructive.

So what do we need to do with diagnoses and labels? I think at least part of the answer comes through communication. We need to talk with one another constructively so that our minds become more open to possibilities. We need to realize that sometimes we may be wrong or have misperceptions. Therefore, we must realize it is prudent not to open fire on those who differ from us by diagnosing or labeling them. Such a process is just too easy and so often wrong.

I believe that individuals who have difficulties in living are many times more stuck than sick. They keep doing what they have always done and while repetition is a good way to learn, it is a less than ideal way to live one's life if the pattern a person is following keeps leading to dead-end streets and frustration. Thus, while merry-go-rounds are fun at the fair, they are fatal as lifestyle strategies.

The challenge in working with people is to invite them to come out from their defenses or standard ways of operating and discuss problems and possibilities with us. As counselors we need to uplift rather than demean; to help people grow, rather than groan. Guilt can be motivating in helping us be aware, but development comes by seeing potentials and not dwelling on disagreements. Acts of forgiveness, kindness, and outreach go much further in bringing about change than actions that preclude discussions. While diagnoses and labels may be necessary at times, we need to remember that people are more complex than the words we use to describe them. Change comes through relationships, not just through rhetoric.

Note. From Gladding, S. T. (2004b, September). Diagnosis, labels, and dialogue. *Counseling Today,* p. 5.

chapter 112

Forgiveness Is Transformational

I am sometimes baffled by clients and colleagues who refuse to consider forgiveness as a part of their lives. My Aunt Mildred was that way. She got into a dispute with my Aunt Elizabeth over God-knows-what and refused to forgive her. She went to her grave at almost 80 still holding onto the grudge and refusing, at the invitation of her minister, to make peace before it was too late.

I loved my Aunt Mildred in many ways. She was generous to me in giving me a ring, and once when our family stopped by the house she shared with my Uncle Alan, she gave each of my children (ages 7, 5, and 3) a $5 bill. She could not only be kind in giving but she was talented too. She was apparently an excellent nurse and I saw her ability to grow tomatoes and other vegetables first hand. In addition, she seemed to get along well with her neighbors and was a connoisseur of antiques. So why she could not forgive my other aunt is beyond me.

In my own life, I have found it easier to forgive others than to forgive myself. I think as human beings we are frail and faulted. We can be petty, angry, and inappropriate. In fact, we can be just plain mean and hateful to each other. I do not always forget those acts of unkindness but I try not to carry grudges. They are just too heavy. I expect more of myself than I do other people. I think my parents helped program that into me but I am the one who crafted the art of trying to live mistake-free.

On most occasions, I live up to my expectations but I still ruminate over two or three things in my life that I wish I had done better or differently. Would my life be different had I not made what I consider to be mistakes? Probably, yes. Would it be better? Not necessarily. Cognitively, I know this. Emotionally, I do not always feel it.

Maybe that is what happened to my aunt. She could not overcome her emotions and in the end they tragically dragged her down. My aunt's example stands out as the antithesis of what we should do. Forgiveness is the balm that transforms a person from a blamer to someone who is free to live with purpose, passion, and possibilities.

chapter 113

The "isms" in Counseling

Alone, she walks slowly home
after a day of giving herself away
at the office to the people
who genuinely need her care and service.
In body, she is as weary
as the cold, night air is dreary,
But she ignores her fatigue and the dark
as she listens to the beat of her heart
which reassures her in the silence
that she has made a difference.

Counseling, like life, is full of "isms." An "ism" has a number of definitions, and its implementation varies in degree from negative to positive. One definition of an "ism" is that it is a distinct doctrine, system, or theory. A complementary definition is that an "ism" may be a practice, process, or action. There are literally dozens of "isms" so I will be able to mention only a few here.

On the negative side of the ledger, racism, the belief that one group of people is superior to another and should be treated better, is an example of a harmful "ism." Terrorism, which is the use of violence to intimidate or coerce others for political or ideological gain, falls into the destructive "isms" category, too. Indeed, many people live in fear of what may befall them as a result of the practices of others. Both of these "isms," racism and terrorism, are among the worst we face in the world today. They have a long history and have plagued the world with barbaric beliefs and horrific acts for hundreds of years. Think of slavery and 9/11, for example. Tragically, they have caused the death, destruction, and ruin of many innocent lives.

A second class of "isms" is somewhat milder in degree, at least on the surface, but is no less destructive in the long run than those just cited.

Two of these "isms," sexism and ageism, stand out because of their prevalence in society. They are not seen as being as blatantly brutal as other categories of injurious "isms." Indeed, they usually are but not at first. However, to discriminate against an individual because of sex, sexual orientation, or age and to deny someone privileges and possibilities when there are no overt reasons to do so is, in the words of Søren Kierkegaard, a "sickness unto death." The beliefs and behaviors that go with this second class of destructive "isms" hurt and slowly destroy persons they are aimed against. Society as a whole is weakened.

As counselors we need to stand up against demeaning and devastating "isms." We all have a stake in each others' lives, for when one of us is hurt or brutalized for reasons beyond that person's control (such as being Asian, Jewish, female, gay, or 70), all of us suffer. The reason is that our humanity transcends our individual identities and an act against one of us is an act against all of us in such circumstances. We are all connected. Unless we consciously fight against the "isms of affliction," we will all be infected with a callous and a caustic spirit that will indeed kill us all ethically, morally, emotionally, and physically.

Yet, despite the deplorability of the "isms" I have just mentioned, there are positive "isms" as well within helping that we need to talk about more and highlight. They are at the heart of counseling, and we must be ever mindful of them.

The first is altruism, that is, unselfish concern for the welfare of others. This kind of unselfishness is a core reason most of us become counselors. We want to help others find their identities, make sound decisions, overcome trying circumstances, and live productive lives. The financial rewards and public recognition for such services are modest at best. Yet, the payoff is an internal satisfaction of having made a difference in the lives of our fellow voyagers. Money and acknowledgment cannot compensate us for the satisfaction and pleasure we derive from these kind acts of helping.

A second productive "ism" that we too seldom celebrate is optimism, the tendency to expect the best and to dwell on the most hopeful outcome in regard to situations. Optimism is a second pillar on which counseling is built as a practice and a profession. It enables us to envision and have a future. It keeps us going. Certainly, if we do not have positive expectation for our clients, we will most likely be of little service to them. In fact, we will be of little help to anyone, including ourselves. Optimism is like a street where realism, encouragement, and possibility meet. Those who travel this road get better instead of bitter.

The final dynamic, good "ism" that I believe we in counseling need to underscore is heroism. Think of the professional counselors who have made a difference in your life or the lives of others: counselors like Fannie Cooley from Tuskeegee, Alabama, or Dick Hackney, from Syracuse, New York. Most likely the professionals you envision have been heroic in the best sense of that word by putting aside personal agendas and acting with courage to assist the individuals who sought their support. Because of their ability and determination to go forward in a quiet, unsung, but productive way, lives were changed and choices were made that enabled and empowered. There is no greater service than to stand in the background and do such unnoticed but significant first-rate deeds.

Therefore, we should, whenever possible, publicly commemorate the helpful and constructive "isms" that make a significant difference in our world. Altruism, optimism, and heroism are bedrock values on which counseling is built. They are qualities that counselors who make a difference embrace and cultivate. In addition, they are characteristics that we must keep emphasizing regardless of where we are in our careers. To dwell on the negative "isms" of our world, such as racism, terrorism, sexism, and ageism is important up to a point but it must be balanced with a look toward and emphasis on the positive "isms." To simply focus on the negatives is to invite discouragement, burnout, frustration, and even anger.

Humanity may yet evolve, as Pierre Teihard de Chardin hypothesized and Abraham Maslow wrote about, to the point where destructive "isms" are eliminated. If that happens, there will be convergence, and the farthest reaches of humankind may be realized. Regardless, we should use the power we have now to promote helpful "isms"—altruism, optimism, and heroism. Interestingly, if the more prosocial "isms" are enlarged, those that are detrimental will lose power. As counselors we work with a variety of clients, ranging from

the anxious to the anorexic,
the behaviorally depressed to the blatantly oppressed,
the careless to the calloused,
the disordered to the disengaged.

Employing productive "isms" in what we do with those who come seeking help may promote within them a vision of "what is" as well as "what can be." If that happens, then there is movement. And if there is movement, we may become like the woman in the opening poem of this chapter, as we reflect with modesty, but with some reassurance, how we have made a difference in the lives of those we have encountered.

Note. From Gladding, S. T. (2004d, December). The "isms" in counseling. *Counseling Today*, p. 5.

chapter 114

Territory Folks Should Stick Together

*I*n the Rogers and Hammerstein musical *Oklahoma* there is a somewhat humorous and energetically performed song and dance about differences and relationships titled "Territory Folks Should Stick Together." It is a production number that initially highlights the dissimilarities between farmers and cowmen, for example, "One man likes to push a plow/The other likes to chase a cow." Yet, given the differences, the song goes on to state: "But that's no reason why they can't be friends." Based on this premise, the lyricist then emphasizes in the refrain that "Territory folks should stick together."

The words in the song are a serious reminder to us within counseling that we have distinctions and overlaps in regard to our emphases in the profession. We see and treat diverse populations, but we do so with a common core of skills, such as those outlined by national accrediting agencies. Given this shared foundation, it is to the benefit of our profession and those we serve to form bonds personally and professionally and to stick together in an association of friendship and vision.

In our collective history, we have sometimes forgotten this fact and regressed into emphasizing how specialties in counseling make us unique and give us an identity. More recently we have begun to stress the universal nature of who we are as counselors in regard to competencies and training. That is a trend that must continue!

Why? Well, there are at least three reasons.

First, stressing our differences instead of our similarities weakens us and upsets us internally. When we perceive specialties and the people in them as fiefdoms not connected with the field as a whole, we may react with hostility instead of with hospitality. We may even become defensive (which often wins athletic events that operate by a zero-sum formula but does not promote positive outcomes in an association or in human relationships). Such a mentality leads to a trading of internal barbs and jabs and a posturing that is pretentious and non-productive. Our various counseling specialties attract dedicated professionals for a number of reasons. Everyone is important and all have a place around the table, for each contributes to the good of the whole regardless of its size or scope.

Thus, we need to hold in check our mindsets as specialists first, for such thinking leads to isolation and alienation because those who practice it begin to believe they are the only island of truth in a turbulent and chaotic world. The result is a focus on the petty as opposed to the profound.

A second reason we need to concentrate initially on what unites us is that it strengthens who we are in the public arena and promotes the common good. A clearer and stronger definition of counseling gives us more power and greater possibilities in passing legislation that supports the welfare of our clients and the profession. Physicians (who also have many specialties) are well known for their success in getting legislation approved nationally and locally. The reason is that they first claim to be doctors and then put emphasis on their special skills. Thus, for the good of the profession of counseling and for the benefit of our clients, I believe we should introduce ourselves initially by using the noun "counselor" or terms such as "professional counselor" or "licensed/certified counselor." Then we should employ one or more adjectives or descriptors that denote our particular niche within the field. Such a stance will hopefully promote counseling, while simultaneously making it clearer to the general public who we are as a group and what we do.

Finally, highlighting the universal nature of counseling will enable the American Counseling Association (ACA) and other entities such as the National Board for Certified Counselors (NBCC), the Council for the Accreditation of Counseling and Related Programs (CACREP), and Chi Sigma Iota, to work together more productively while not distracting any of them from their distinct missions. An example of such collaboration occurred in Indiana where ACA and NBCC worked with other entities, including the Indiana Counseling Association, to prevent the restriction of test use. Collaboration of this nature has also happened in states where counselor licensure has been enacted.

So, in a way we are all Oklahomans—cowmen, cowwomen, merchants, and farmers—in the territory of counseling. We have a choice to continue to be cooperative or to be in conflict. Personally and professionally, I believe the decision is clear in regard to its results. As the poet Maya Angelou has written in her poem *Friends,* "We are more alike my friend, than we are unalike."

Or to put it in a more prosaic form from the Chick-Fil-A Super Hero Cows, who advertise for this restaurant "United we stand, divided we're steak."

Being more unified in our attitudes, focus, and identity will enable us to be more of a creative and dynamic force in promoting change and competence within and outside of the profession of counseling. It is a position we cannot afford to shrink from or to shirk. Rather, it is one we must continue to emphasize with courage and conviction. The reason is simple. Our futures as generalists and specialists depend on it, as do the futures of those we serve!

Note. From Gladding, S. T. (2004a, August). Territory folks should stick together. *Counseling Today*, p. 5.

chapter 115

Counseling or Counselling:
Internationally Speaking

The tsunami that occurred in the Indian Ocean on December 26, 2004, was a tragic event. Those who experienced its horrors first-hand suffered severe loss and trauma. For some, the grief and the recovery from the devastation will continue for years. For others, the events of the day will never go away as they relive them post-traumatically.

Witnessing the terror of the tidal wave on television, most of us were filled with a feeling of surreal shock. We saw raging waters cluttered with debris sweep people across beaches and through streets which minutes before had been calm. Before this event many of us did not know what a tsunami was, let alone how to spell it. Now the word and its power are etched indelibly in our minds. Many of us have given aid materially, as we have in other tragedies. Out of calamity we have recognized anew the fragile nature of life and our interconnectedness. As counselors we are a part of those we encounter directly as well as those we come to know through the news. That includes individuals in our profession around the world.

Tradition has it (whether true or not) that the spelling of the words *counseling* and *counselor* is primarily due to a pioneer in the profession, Frank Parsons. He was employed in a number of jobs, one of them being a "counsellor-at-law." Parsons liked the sound of the word *counsellor*. Therefore, when he changed vocations and began working with young people, he spelled the word *counselor* with one "l" to make sure those whom he knew did not get his present work confused with his former profession.

In the United States we have inherited the spelling of *counselor* and *counseling* with one "l" and everything that goes with it. As professional counselors in numerous specialties, we are not confused with attorneys. However, since the American public seems to love the word "counselor," we sometimes have to explain how we differ from the people in our country who add prefixes to the word such as *camp, carpet, financial*, and *pest control*. That means we often have to explain what *counseling* is.

Professionals in other countries who have not imported our spelling do not have the same difficulty. The reason is that *counsellor* is spelled with two "l"s. Now I am not sure if they are sometimes mistaken for attorneys, but I think it might be better for those of us in the United States to reconsider the spelling of our professional name.

The reasons for such a consideration are twofold. First, by spelling our title as counsellors instead of counselors, we will be much more in step with our fellow professionals in other countries. Often, we want the world to imitate the United States. However, at least in this case, we might be wise to adopt the spelling of the rest of the English-speaking world. Counselling is a worldwide phenomenon. We have much to learn from counsellors in Africa, Asia, Australia, Europe, and the rest of the Americas.

A second reason for changing the spelling of our name is recognition. Attorneys usually put the words *at law* after the word *counsellor.* They even hyphenate the term *counsellor-at-law.* On the other hand, any modifier we might place before or after the word *counsellor,* would clearly distinguish us from those in the practice of law. Even if we did not add prefixes or suffixes, it might be more gratifying to be mistaken for a lawyer than an exterminator (although there are those who would beg to differ).

So, even though one letter seems like a small distinction, it could make a big difference. By becoming counsellors instead of counselors, we might become more international in our outlook and more connected with our fellow professionals. Therefore, instead of just promoting the profession of counseling from the inside out, we might truly become more collaborative. In addition, any confusion that now hinders the public's understanding of our profession might be reduced. Who knows? Public recognition and use of counselors might increase. So, think about it. Is the "American Counselling Association" something we want in our future?

Regardless, let us keep those whose lives have been shattered by both natural and man-made events uppermost in our thoughts and our actions. It is in reaching out compassionately that we can help them recover. An extra letter in the words *counselor* and *counseling* may not make a "l" of a lot of difference. However, being generous to those with whom we share this planet can be life-saving and transformational. As counselors or counsellors, let us open up and respond by giving to other who are in crisis with graciousness and substance.

Note. From Gladding, S. T. (2005c, April). Counseling or counselling: Internationally speaking. *Counseling Today,* p. 5.

chapter 116

Why Counseling?

*I*t came out of the air and into our minds like a nightmare. People and places we knew disappeared in a matter of minutes. It was surreal, horrific, and anguishing. Yet, there it was before us. We could see it, hear it, and experience it to the marrow of our bones from the television and radio news reports. The event, of course, was the terrorist attacks on the World Trade Center and the Pentagon on September 11, 2001, a landmark day that touched our lives profoundly at the time and continues to impact them even now, especially those in the military.

So why recall the day in a commentary about counseling? Certainly there is relevance in regard to the anxiety, grief, and a torrent of other human emotions we saw displayed before us and that will remain indelibly etched in our minds. Similarly, we saw need in its rawest form from the pictures that were laid out before us. Furthermore, we realized then as now that people are multidimensional and we must take care of the affective as well as the behavioral and cognitive. However, I think there is more to the event than any of these first dominant thoughts. Rather, it is beyond the obvious that I think we find answers, or least the beginnings of answers, to why counseling is needed in our time.

The first reason is care. In the aftermath of the destructive scenes from New York and Virginia, we saw acts of kindness, concern, and even heroism as people helped people in ways that were well beyond the expected. Such moments stand as monuments before us as we think about them. They are inspiring and point to the greatness within persons that often goes unnoticed or undisplayed.

Yet, after such important physical behaviors, what? There is, I would propose, a need then to debrief and deal with the emotions that soon follow times of trauma. In our day we recognize posttraumatic stress disorder and its debilitating impact on those who have gone through crisis. While sincere and sensitive people can and sometimes succeed in displaying what Carl Rogers described as the "necessary and sufficient conditions" appropriate for counseling, too often individuals with a desire to be helpful fail because they are at a loss as to what to do, when, and how.

It is counselors who can step into such a vacuum and fill it. Clinical skills can go a long way in assisting others. They make coping possible until intra- and inter-stability are achieved. It is the right kind of care that makes a difference in people's lives, and counselors are equipped to provide such. Thus, at times like these, counselors function in essential ways for those who have experienced disaster and trauma either directly or on a second-hand level.

A second quality counselors and counseling offer is the possibility to create and make choices and changes in one's life that were not previously considered. When emotions are stirred up, they are often accompanied by a wish to explore new ways of being. Counseling is germane to such moments, and again counselors have the skills and abilities to guide individuals in such a process.

Being creative is sometimes thought of as mysterious and only reserved for a few special people. Mihaly Csikszentmihalyi, the author of *Flow,* has discovered, however, that anyone has the possibility to learn to be creative. People may do so by engaging in such simple things as minimizing or maximizing a response, learning a new behavior, substituting or altering ways of responding, and reversing or rearranging what they do and when. The possibilities are great and the payoffs are rewarding. Counseling offers creativity to clients in the forms of altering behaviors, emotions, or thoughts. Sometimes small change, as Stephen deShazer notes, is all that is needed. Such a service is invaluable when old responses are either destructive or nonproductive.

Finally, counseling offers hope in times that seem hopeless and at moments when many feel helpless. Too often, people view events from a distance that is disconcerting and prevents them from connecting with anything but the chaos that surrounds them. In such situations, there is a tendency to disconnect and to feel depressed or a propensity to propose short-term or simple solutions to long-term and complex problems. Counseling, at its best, prevents such tendencies by focusing on the possible and not just the immediate problem. In counseling, solutions that go beyond the immediate emerge if the process is carried out right. Thus, life beyond trauma emerges.

It is this quality of hope that helps connect people together in productive ways and allies counseling with other helping professions, especially those that deal holistically with people. Hope gives individuals who have been through stress a way to address both who they are now and what they will be. Hope provides a basis for moving on in life and not staying stuck in a day or event that was destructive. Without hope, there is little life. There is a lack of purpose, too. It is counseling that can not only calm but call individuals to a better way of being by envisioning the best and not the beast within them and others, regardless of background.

In all of our lives, there are days of fear and times of terror. These times usually do not strike in such a devastating matter as those of September 11th. Yet, they are there. Death, like life, is a part of our existence. The unexpected, as well as the predictable, are a part of our environment. We cannot escape these facts, nor should we try. There are amusements and parks that offer temporary reprieve should we need it.

Yet, counseling offers more. It looks at reality and accepts what is, but it doesn't stay there. Counseling offers three ways of dealing with what stands before us. It offers *care* in the form of knowing how to respond and when to act. It offers *creativity* in helping people put their lives back together in a way that is ever new, ever changing, and productive. Finally, it offers *hope* both in what we can be and who we can help others become. The holistic view of humankind that counseling offers goes beyond the mundane and the tragic that all too often fill the world. The possible and productive side of counseling call out to a world in chaos that there is hope that comes in the form of listening, understanding, and responding in ways that bridge gaps instead of create them.

Counseling is not the only profession that has something positive to say to the situations we face as a people. However, it is a voice that speaks to growth and goodness. In a world that is disturbed and distracted by the sounds of demigods and sometimes the demonic, a voice like ours is needed.

Points to Ponder

1. How have you seen various aspects of counseling touch the lives of people in your community? What do you think the founders of the profession would think if they could see it now?

2. Diagnoses are given to some people in society like labels are put on clothes. Why is such a practice harmful? What would you suggest be done instead of diagnosing? On the other hand, what positive purpose does diagnosing serve?

3. There are literally dozens of "isms" worldwide. Besides the "isms" named in this section, think of two more and how they relate to counseling. Why should "isms" not be seen as all negative or all positive?

Section | Fourteen

TERMINATION

Death caught my father by surprise.
He had other activities planned for that April day
like weeding the garden and listening to a Braves' game.
Yet startled as he was
he had the presence of mind
to empty his pockets
before the ambulance came.
I am sure he did not know that he had suffered a triple aneurysm
(I doubt he would have cared).
My father was accepting
he loved plants and people, especially his family,
he was aware of his own mortality.
In sadness
I find relief
(and even comfort)
in knowing how well he lived.

The end of an event is usually not the climax of the experience. Yet, termination is important in counseling because it offers closure. Too often termination is minimized or neglected. The result is that learning that has occurred prior to the end of the counseling experience may be lost.

In this section, "The Quilt" illustrates how a proper ending can have a profound impact on a client. "Hair" goes beyond focusing just on the client to show how we as counselors are affected by the end of life and relationships. "On Grief and Gratitude" deals with personal loss also and how we respond when death is within the family. This section ends with a little humor and the optimism of Gordon Allport in "Always Becoming."

|305

chapter 117

The Quilt

I once worked with an elderly woman. She had had a terrible life and was destitute and distraught. She was also dying. The facts of her life were pretty plain and straightforward, but she had not been able to come to terms with her situation or get relief from the troubles that had surrounded her. In the midst of a rather depressing session, I asked an unusual question because the obvious ones were not working.

"So what do you do for fun?"

Fun was not a theme running through this woman's life, and to introduce it seemed a bit bizarre, but after looking at me with rather sobering eyes, she said, "I sew."

"I don't," I replied, "but I know that sewing is an art, and I've always admired people who could do it. Would you bring some of your sewing into the sessions?"

She agreed to, and the next time we met she did just that, spending most of the session telling me about her work. I then asked if she was still actively engaged in sewing. "Yes," she responded. As we talked, she came up with an idea of sewing a square patch of cloth that represented something important in her life that she wanted to resolve. From then on she came in with patches that represented different aspects of her life, many of which were adverse, such as the death of one of her children, her divorce, the loss of her energy as she grew older, and the pain of poverty. There were a few positive patches that she brought in also, like the memory of a special friend from adolescence and a trip she had once made to Chicago.

One day she came without a patch but with a brown paper grocery bag. I kidded her that she must have sewn all night. In all seriousness, she replied that she had. Then she reached into the sack and brought out a small patchwork quilt. It contained all of her pain and the few bright spots in her life. It was not elegant, but it was beautiful. At the top, she had embroidered the word "PEACE" in blue thread on a white background.

"I'm at peace," she said. "I can now face life or death with serenity."

A few months later she died. I was saddened by her passing, but I knew she had left her bitterness behind. Through her art of sewing, she had made connections in her life that allowed her to grow and accept herself as well as find meaning in her existence.

chapter 118

Hair

As a graduate student I went to New York and saw the Broadway play "Hair." But that's not what this story is all about. Instead, it involves a young woman I worked with in counseling. She was gaunt when I first saw her, dressed in an oversized white tee shirt, blue jeans, and tennis shoes. However, her bony features and baggy clothes did not take me aback nearly as much as the fact that she was bald. I am sure my face must have given away my surprise, for she said immediately on meeting me, "My hair fell out last Tuesday. Radiation treatments will do that to you."

"I don't normally see women without their hair," I said. "I must admit the sight of you has caught me off guard. You have cancer?"

"Yes. It's in the early stages, and I intend to beat it. But I need some help. I need an ally."

Thus, we began with an explanation and admission on her part and an acknowledgment and inquiry on mine. We worked that summer and into three more seasons. Hair became the least of my concerns. Her strength and ability to function dominated my thoughts when I was with her.

I would love to say that she won the battle for her life and that her hair came back. Neither event happened. However, from our sessions I learned a lot about courage and grace. I watched her fade but not without a fight that was heroic.

To this day, whenever I look at a young woman with flowing thick hair I think of that client. I realize that it is beneath such a rich exterior that the essence of a person lies. Hair sometimes hides the beauty of a person or tragically prevents it from developing.

chapter 119

Avoiding Permanent Termination:
Self-Care and SIFLs

*A*lthough my tenure in the Army was rather brief, I learned a lot. One was about the importance of self-care and what happens when someone loses that battle. In the Army, the opposite of self-care came in the form of an acronym known as a SIFL (self-inflicted frontal lobotomy). A person could get a SIFL several ways, but the most common was to become sleep deprived.

In the Army, it was easy to achieve a sleep deprivation state whether one intended to or not. The reason is that in armed forces training there is an emphasis on maneuvers which often take place at night. That would be okay, except the next day soldiers do not usually get time off. Instead, they get more training, some of which is not overly stimulating (i.e., it is dull).

When at Fort Lee, Virginia, I witnessed several SIFLs. I was stationed in the back of the classroom where these events happened, so I had one of the best observation posts available. Usually, SIFLs were afternoon events. Right after lunch was a prime time when there was a natural tendency to be drowsy and some soldiers felt lousy and fatigued from running around in the woods the previous night. Mid-afternoon was another frequent point in time. Regardless, SIFLs were most likely to happen when there was a lecture on something rather dull such as "Supplying Socks to Master Sergeants" or "How to Make Friends With Furry Animals When Trapped Behind Enemy Lines." In these cases, the person who was overly tired would temporarily begin to lose control of his or her body and weave back and forth. Most would catch themselves and try with all their might to sit up straight and pay attention. They were often successful once or twice but finally some would surrender to the dark side (i.e., they would close their eyes), and at that moment it was usually all over. The previous sways and drifts would turn into smashing dives and their heads would come crashing down on the metal desks before them.

The sound was distinctive. It was a loud thud that startled everyone in the room including the lecturer, who might be droning on about sock sizes or different types of squirrels, depending on the topic at hand. In any case, friends of the SIFL victim would usually escort or carry the person from the room and to the infirmary. These escorts were grateful that they were getting out of class, but they usually felt sorry for their fallen comrade. Sometimes the victim showed up later in formation with a bandaged head. On one occasion we never saw the soldier again.

The point is that no one is able to fight the inevitable. Fatigue, whether of a physical or a compassionate nature, eventually will cause individuals to fall out. Most of us as counselors do not land on top of steel desks. However, when we are overstressed we do not land on our feet either. Rather, we become more irritable, less open, disgruntled, cynical, or just plain worn out. Any of these states of mind bode ill for the clients we see and for our interactions with colleagues.

Counseling demands that we take care of ourselves regardless of the environments in which we are immersed. Otherwise, we will give ourselves self-inflicted wounds which may or may not heal in time. These injuries may inhibit us from being the professional helpers we are striving to become.

chapter 120

On Grief and Gratitude

*I*t occurred unexpectedly. The voice mail message was from the veterinarian. "Eli has had a stroke and is struggling. He is not responding to treatment. I may have to put him to sleep. Please call me." I looked at my watch. It was 6:15 p.m., and the clinic had closed for the day. I was in Florida, 600 miles away from North Carolina. I had no choice but to wait until the following morning to find out the fate of my 16-year-old dog. Heavy-hearted, I walked back to my motel. I knew the night would be long and the outcome would most likely be what I feared the most.

Eli had come into my life when I was in my early 30s. He was a blessing. As I moved through the ranks of academic circles and up and down the East Coast, Eli was my steady companion and confidant. He accepted Claire, my wife, and each of our three children as they entered his life. He was open to change and adaptable to new experiences. Even in old age he appeared to enjoy our family, and always took his naps near us or on piles of laundry. Now he was struggling for his life, and I was helpless to help him.

The next day I called the vet as early as possible, and the doctor informed me of Eli's death. My heart sank, my throat grew thick, and my eyes welled up with tears. I tried to speak, but my voice kept cracking, and there were long pauses in between words. "We'll save his body for you" were the final words of the conversation. So when I arrived back in Winston-Salem, I went to pick up Eli for his last ride home. That afternoon, with care, I buried him next to the backyard fence he had loved to patrol. Each child and Claire said good-bye to the dog that had shared his life with us. The funeral was bittersweet, filled with fond memories and deep sorrow.

Pets and people come into our lives in many ways. The experiences we have with them often make us more sensitive and open to the world. In death, there is a sadness but also a celebration. We become more aware of who we are in relationships as memories mingle with tears. Letting go of that which was and those we love is difficult. Saying hello to emptiness, the unknown, and new beginnings is painful. Amidst it all and above it all, however, we can be grateful. Even in loss there is life. It is the life of having been. Such a realization gives us hope for the future. If there have been good old days, there may be good new days as well. As the late Dag Hammarskjold (1965) said in his book *Markings,* "For all that has been—Thanks! To all that shall be—Yes!"

chapter 121

Always Becoming

*T*he phrase "always becoming" is attributed to Gordon Allport. He believed people were continuously developing, and so do I. Even at termination there is growth, although we and the clients with whom we work do not always see it clearly.

In my quest to become a counselor, it took me many years of study to obtain the necessary degrees. The process became so long that when friends would ask my father what I was going to be when I finished, he would quip, "He's going to be old!"

Actually, my father knew, as did I, that the termination of study would lead to a graduation and to a new life and lifestyle.

We, as counselors, often have difficulty with endings. Beginnings and renewing are much more enjoyable. However, every exit is also an entrance. So as you finish this book be aware that experiences turned into memories make a difference. New chapters in life begin when old ones come to a close.

Points to Ponder

1. Recall and write down important milestones and memories in your life. What have you done to resolve those situations that were difficult transitions for you? What are some ways you could come to terms with them?

2. Think of positive traits that you have admired in someone who has died. How could you incorporate some of these qualities into your own life?

3. What do you want your legacy to be as a person? As a counselor? Write a paragraph about what you would want others to say about you.

EPILOGUE

Finishing a book that is both personal and professional in nature, like this one, can produce a plethora of thoughts and emotions. For example, you may feel validated or energized as well as disappointed that the end of the text was reached too soon or that certain situations were not covered. I have similar thoughts and feelings. Such bittersweet responses are natural and to be expected.

My hope is that some of the stories you have read in these pages will influence you positively and help you become a bit different than before. Furthermore, it is also my wish that you will carry some of the stories forward into your life and that they may enrich and delight you as a part of your memory. Finally, I hope that you will see counseling as a profession that is filled with a great variety of experiences where your skills, insights, and creativity will be tested in ways that will spark both your growth and that of your clients. If any of these three experiences happens, then your completion of these pages may lead to new beginnings, including the writing and telling of your own stories as a counselor. Who could ask for more?

NOTES

[1]From "Drumbeat," by S. T. Gladding, 1993, Unpublished manuscript. Copyright 1993 by Samuel T. Gladding.

[2]From "Small Change," by S. T. Gladding, 1996, Unpublished manuscript. Copyright 1996 by Samuel T. Gladding.

[3]From *Reality Sits in a Green Cushioned Chair* (p. 17), by S. T. Gladding, 1976, Atlanta, GA: Collegiate Press. Copyright 1976 by S. T. Gladding. Reprinted with permission.

[4]From "Patchwork," by S. T. Gladding, 1974, *The Personnel and Guidance Journal, 53,* p. 39. Copyright 1974 by the American Counseling Association. Reprinted with permission.

[5]From "A Snapshot of Tim in Fourth Grade," by S. T. Gladding, 2000, Unpublished manuscript. Copyright 2000 by Samuel T. Gladding.

[6]From *Group Work: A Counseling Specialty* (3rd ed., p. 196), by S. T. Gladding, 1999, Upper Saddle River, NJ: Prentice Hall. Copyright 1999 by S. T. Gladding. Reprinted with permission.

[7]From *Family Therapy: History, Theory and Practice* (2nd ed., p. 199), by S. T. Gladding, 1998, Upper Saddle River, NJ: Prentice Hall. Copyright 1998 by S. T. Gladding. Reprinted with permission.

[8]From *Group Work: A Counseling Specialty* (3rd ed., p. 44), by S. T. Gladding, 1999, Upper Saddle River, NJ: Prentice Hall. Copyright 1999 by S. T. Gladding. Reprinted with permission.

[9]From "Reflections on a Professional Friendship," by S. T. Gladding, 1989, *Journal of Humanistic Education and Development, 27,* pp. 190–191. Copyright 1989 by the American Counseling Association. Reprinted with permission.

[10]From "Change," by S. T. Gladding, 2005, Unpublished manuscript. Copyright 2005 by Samuel T. Gladding.

[11]From "Alexandria Reflections," by S. T. Gladding, 2008, Unpublished manuscript. Copyright 2008 by Samuel T. Gladding.

REFERENCES

Gladding, S. T. (1974). Patchwork. *The Personnel and Guidance Journal, 53,* 39.

Gladding, S. T. (1976). *Reality sits in a green cushioned chair.* Atlanta, GA: Collegiate Press.

Gladding, S. T. (1989). Reflections on a professional friendship. *Journal of Humanistic Education and Development, 27,* 190–191.

Gladding, S. T. (1998). *Family therapy: History, theory and practice* (2nd ed.). Upper Saddle River, NJ: Prentice Hall.

Gladding, S. T. (1999). *Group work: A counseling specialty* (3rd ed.). Upper Saddle River, NJ: Prentice Hall.

Gladding, S. T. (2002). Reflections on counseling after the crisis. In G. R. Walz & C. J. Kirkman (Eds.), *Helping people cope with tragedy and grief* (pp. 9–12). Greensboro, NC: CAPS.

Gladding, S. T. (2004a, August). Territory folks should stick together. *Counseling Today,* p. 5.

Gladding, S. T. (2004b, September). Diagnosis, labels, and dialogue. *Counseling Today,* p. 5.

Gladding, S. T. (2004c, October). The leader as a catalyst and servant. *Counseling Today,* p. 5.

Gladding, S. T. (2004d, December). The "isms" in counseling. *Counseling Today,* p. 5.

Gladding, S. T. (2005a, January). Counseling in an age of chaos. *Counseling Today,* p. 5.

Gladding, S. T. (2005b, February). The right to struggle. *Counseling Today,* p. 5.

Gladding, S. T. (2005c, April). Counseling or counselling: Internationally speaking. *Counseling Today,* p. 5.

Gladding, S. T. (2005d, May). Counseling as a quiet resolution. *Counseling Today,* p. 5.

References

Goldin, E., Bordan, T., Araoz, D. L., Gladding, S. T., Kaplan, D., Krumboltz, J., & Lazarus, A. (2006). Humor in counseling: Leader perspectives. *Journal of Counseling & Development, 84,* 397–405.

Hammarskjold, D. (1965). *Markings.* New York: Knopf.

Lerner, A. (1978). *Poetry as therapy.* New York: Pergamon Press.